"What if everything we've bee... ...g? Mekdes Haddis forces us to confront the dangers inherent in the power, privilege, and metrics of Western missions and invites us to a better way forward. We have not listened long enough or well enough to Black and Brown Christian leaders about missions, and that's to our shame. It's time we move from Western notions of transactional relationships within the missions field to pursue relational mutuality that can be championed by anyone, especially those in the Global South. If you're interested in missions, start with this book!"

Michelle Ami Reyes, vice president of the Asian American Christian Collaborative and author of *Becoming All Things*

"*A Just Mission* is a necessary read for white evangelical churches and organizations that continue to perpetuate colonialism and imperialism through overseas mission trips."

Ekemini Uwan, public theologian and cohost of *Truth's Table* podcast

"It is long past time for the church to learn about God's missional heart from African and non-Western sisters and brothers. Mekdes Abebe Haddis has given us a gift in *A Just Mission*. Through her personal story of faith as an Ethiopian woman, she tells the truth about harm that has been done in the missional endeavors of Western Christianity, and calls the church to a more faithful future of missions for the current age."

Irwyn L. Ince Jr., author of *The Beautiful Community*

"In her book *A Just Mission*, the African missionary Mekdes Haddis has beautifully expressed what many African diaspora theologians and scholars have felt but failed to ink. Mekdes gently but firmly reminds readers about the unconscious and yet devastating practices of Western missionaries whose gospel was wrapped in colonial flags and cultural biases that did not value indigenous people as fully human or view their cultures as redeemable. Unfortunately, this sense of cultural and racial superiority continues to blind the Western church from seeing diaspora theologians and Bible scholars as cultural teachers and brokers as well as partners in reaching the post-Christian West and strengthening the growing church in the Global South."

Celestin Musekura, founder and global ambassador for African Leadership and Reconciliation Ministries

"Reading this powerful book reminded me that the forces upholding the existing missions model in America are strong and rooted in ideology, economics, and histories that are hundreds of years old. Mekdes Haddis gives us the gift of a rich resource to form our repentance and changed behavior as we work together to build a just mission."

Dennae Pierre, codirector of the Crete Collective, City to City North America, and the Surge Network

"'Wounds from a friend can be trusted,' and Mekdes Abebe Haddis gives a direct yet loving rebuke to the Western approach to global missions. With clarity and conviction, this book helps readers see beyond biases and blind spots to embrace a mission that elevates and humanizes all people. Haddis calls for relationship and reciprocity, mutuality and mutual respect, and a move away from saviorism to better reflect the Savior. In this book you will discover the beauty of a justice-seeking, gospel-advancing global church."

Peter Greer, president and CEO of HOPE International, author of *The Gift of Disillusionment*

"Western mission leaders must ask themselves, 'Will what got us here get us there?' It is time to consider new, just, alternative options to help us get to the next 'there.' We need a recalibration of pathways to get different laborers. If we learned anything from the woman's story at the well in John 4, it is that established leaders can at times miss the contribution of different people commissioned by God. I believe Mekdes Haddis calls us to open our eyes to embrace a just paradigm of different missionaries."

Alejandro Mandes, executive director of the EFCA All People Ministry

"Mekdes Haddis's hope and love for the Western church shines through full words of critique, rebuke, and correction. Haddis holds in tension the real harm done by white saviorism and white nationalism in evangelical practice with the real transformation and repair Jesus offers. Church leaders and congregants alike would do well to read *A Just Mission* in community."

Kathy Khang, author of *Raise Your Voice: Why We Stay Silent and How to Speak Up*

MEKDES HADDIS

FOREWORD BY LATASHA MORRISON

A JUST

MISSION

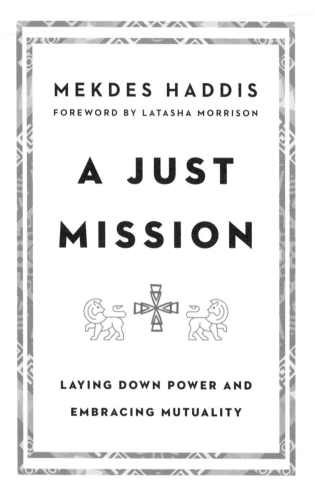

LAYING DOWN POWER AND

EMBRACING MUTUALITY

An imprint of InterVarsity Press
Downers Grove, Illinois

InterVarsity Press
P.O. Box 1400 | Downers Grove, IL 60515-1426
ivpress.com | email@ivpress.com

InterVarsity Press® is the publishing division of InterVarsity Christian Fellowship/USA®. For more information, visit intervarsity.org.

Scripture quotations have been taken from the Christian Standard Bible®, Copyright © 2017 by Holman Bible Publishers. Used by permission. Christian Standard Bible® and CSB® are federally registered trademarks of Holman Bible Publishers.

While any stories in this book are true, some names and identifying information may have been changed to protect the privacy of individuals.

The publisher cannot verify the accuracy or functionality of website URLs used in this book beyond the date of publication.

Cover design and image composite: David Fassett
Interior design: Daniel van Loon

ISBN 978-1-5140-0367-1 (print) | ISBN 978-1-5140-0368-8 (digital)

Printed in the United States of America ⊖

Library of Congress Cataloging-in-Publication Data
Names: Haddis, Mekdes Abebe, 1984- author.
Title: A just mission: laying down power and embracing mutuality / Mekdes
   Haddis; foreword by Latasha Morrison
Description: Downers Grove, IL: InterVarsity Press, [2022] | Includes
   bibliographical references.
Identifiers: LCCN 2022019880 (print) | LCCN 2022019881 (ebook) | ISBN
   9781514003671 (print) | ISBN 9781514003688 (digital)
Subjects: LCSH: Missions–Theory. | Christianity and culture. |
   Postcolonial theology.
Classification: LCC BV2063 .H23 2022 (print) | LCC BV2063 (ebook) | DDC
   266–dc23/eng/20220613
LC record available at https://lccn.loc.gov/2022019880
LC ebook record available at https://lccn.loc.gov/2022019881
A catalog record for this book is available from the Library of Congress.

29 28 27 26 25 24 23 22 | 13 12 11 10 9 8 7 6 5 4 3 2 1

THIS BOOK IS DEDICATED TO MY FATHER,

Abebe Haddis,

who instilled in me a love for cultures through reading,

music, and travel. Gashe, here is a book published with

your name in it, telling our story with our Creator

the way we always knew it to be. And to my mother,

Amsalu Assefa (Etetye), your love is unmatched and

has inspired me to search and find the One who

is the source of it all. Without him this book

would have been a clanging cymbal.

CONTENTS

FOREWORD

WHEN I WENT TO RWANDA ON A MISSION TRIP, I was struck by meeting Rwandans with names like Susan, Sara, Patrice, Calvin. It left me wondering why they had English names. I later found out that these were their Christian baptism names. When they accepted Christ as their personal Savior, they were also given "Christian names." In reality the names given to them were just English names and had nothing to do with Christ. The irony is that their Rwandan names were actually true Christian names; some of their meanings were "blessed of God" or "light of God."

Defining Christianity by English names signified to me that something had gone wrong in the way Christ was introduced to them. They were being taught that God wasn't in their culture, and they must conform to whiteness to be closer to God. That is one example of the damage that Western mission work has done to Black and Brown people as it preached that imported Western hair styles, foods, music, language, and clothing are better than what God has naturally given them in their context.

A Just Mission is a book that can be a game changer for the American church. If it's embraced, it can help reframe our ideologies around mission and help us move forward. But if it's ignored because it makes some people feel uncomfortable, the American church will greatly miss out. Mekdes Haddis uses a bridge-building approach to a broken mission system. She not only talks about the problem but offers solutions by providing historical factors to help institutions correct past mistakes. Her focus in contextualizing theology is so key to understanding how we have hurt culture in our mission movement. In our attempts to do good, we have dropped bombs in communities and left them to pick up the pieces. When we don't see God in other cultures but instead assume our culture is supreme and the right way to do something, we disrupt his good work in creation and damage the foundation of a diverse global church. If American Christians will listen to this message, it will reshape not just the mission movement but Western Christianity for the better.

Mekdes is the perfect person to talk about this complex subject in a restorative and redeeming manner. Her writing lifts up those who have been harmed but also creates a way forward for those who have done the harm to correct their mistakes. This book not only states the problem but provides the solutions that need to be considered to build a more inclusive missional movement. Bridge building is key in empowering and educating mission organizations to do mission justly and to rebuild God's kingdom with his whole body in mind. *A Just Mission* is a much-needed book for the church to see the world through the lenses of reconciliation and justice.

INTRODUCTION

Until the lion learns how to write,
every story will glorify the hunter.

J. Nozipo Maraire

THE SELFLESS ACT OF CHRIST'S sacrifice on the cross made a way for individuals to be reconciled not only with the Father but also with one another. God's heart for his children is that they flourish in diversity and unify around the majesty of his glory. Sadly our sin has put a wedge in the global body's ability to worship together. One particular group of Christians has claimed authority over the rest of the body and how Christianity should look for the rest of humankind.

For decades the Western church has been the largest missionary-sending agency in the world. In fact, the saying "from the West to the rest" was coined to describe this phenomenon. Yet those days are long gone, as Christianity is booming in the Global South and migration has enabled missions to be from everywhere to everywhere. So why haven't mission organizations and churches of the West embraced this new reality? Why haven't they restructured their institutions to reflect the cultural diversity of the global church by allowing everybody to take part in leadership? As the American evangelical church lags behind on issues of racial justice and equality, the mission movement it leads is on the cusp of dying from irrelevance.

As protests of white supremacy grow, secular organizations such as Black Lives Matter and No White Saviors are creating greater awareness of the goer's need to seek an approach of mutuality. In response, the Western church has started to grapple with finding a redemption from her role in creating a global problem by seeking mutuality.

Yet the question remains: Is mutuality even possible when the Global South, where the fastest-growing churches exist, is full of Brown and Black people yet the largest mission organizations are not led by them? The absence of global leaders representing different cultures, languages, and ethnic groups in the boardrooms of these so-called global organizations creates a problem in accomplishing the most important work Jesus Christ has given his church. How do we as global Christians work together to reach the world with the gospel effectively in a manner that contextualizes theology, restores justice, and mobilizes the next generation for the harvest that awaits?

The Western church must undertake a significant effort to understand the harmful effects of its mission legacy. Its tendency to conflate mission with colonization affects far more than individuals, reaching whole cultures. These people groups have been economically and culturally shaped by Western ideologies that leave them handicapped, which has created a vicious cycle of dependency on the white savior to come fix the problems the Western church created. I have met many enthusiastic mission practitioners who rave about their ability to work mutually with local people to create structures that fit the local context. While I applaud their efforts and appreciate their heart, I wonder if they truly understand how their local partners would define "mutuality." If they did, I am certain they would be far less eager to celebrate their ability to be in mutual leadership and more frustrated by what was being asked of them.

As an Ethiopian American who has lived in both countries and speaks both Amharic and English, I have had plenty of opportunities to sit on both sides of the aisle and listen to unfiltered and unhindered discussions of mutuality from my colleagues. I can tell you there is a lot my African colleagues wish they could do but are prevented from undertaking because of what feels like an "iron fist" imposed on them by organizations that need to keep donors happy. When it boils down to it, for missions to be completely true and helpful in context, indigenous leaders need to be fully in charge of decision making on the ground and in the boardroom. In most cases, however, this is far from reality.

Usually, someone living in a First-World country comes up with goals and metrics that are impossible to meet without sidestepping the needs of the very people the mission is designed to love and care for. The West's contribution to the global mission movement is a necessary evil, a painful realization Western mission leaders must live with. This is not something indigenous leaders can discuss with those who consider themselves "mutual partners." This division and power dynamic reflects what's happening in the segregation of churches here in America, where white church-planting organizations struggle to plant multiethnic churches for lack of mutuality. The only difference is those in the United States can say no to the iron fist, while leaders of the Global South cannot. Their people's livelihood depends on their ability to get aid from Western organizations. This tension needs to be discussed not only from a US perspective but also in how it manifests in the global mission movement.

As someone who lives in both worlds, I offer a different approach to mutuality, one that gives Western Christians, missionaries, and church leaders a lens through which to view the past accurately so they can identify what's broken in their institutions and fix it. In order to build a collaborative and vibrant missional movement for the next generation, we must move from listening to taking costly action. My goal in this book is to help move us from a heavily transactional relationship in the mission movement to a relational mutuality that can be owned, championed, and led by everyone in the global church. In order to break the hierarchy of elitism in the institutionalized mission movement, we must address issues of white supremacy, decolonize our faith, and institute restorative justice. Only then can we truly build a mutually beneficial relationship and find a common strategy to reach the lost with the hope only God offers: salvation through his Son Jesus Christ.

MY JOURNEY INTO MISSION

Growing up in Addis Ababa, Ethiopia, I developed an understanding of the West from my parents, who gently introduced me to Western culture as a way of preparing me to succeed in the global market. My dad traveled throughout Ethiopia as an investment banker who focused on development and aid. Talk of a hopeful and beautiful Ethiopia was always present in our home. My dad would tell us of the progress being made by the coffee farmers who had received loans from his bank, showing us the fresh coffee bean samples that we delighted to watch him process until they made it into his cup. His position allowed him to observe our people moving toward economic growth, and not once did I hear him describe Ethiopia as a home of the voiceless or hopeless. I grew up with a sense of pride and dignity, a feeling that my home was whole and complete in itself.

On weekends my father took my siblings and me to the British Council Library. We could pick out any book we wanted, and if we managed to finish reading it before the weekend was over, my father let us watch action movies with him. It was the highlight of my weekend after not having him around most of the week. My dad loves music as well as books, and he pulled out an old-school record player from time to time to play Elvis, Nat King Cole, and Kenny Rogers. He told us stories of the people he met as he traveled to Europe or Asia, which instilled in us an early desire to travel the world and meet all kinds of people ourselves. The exposure was subtle but intentional; he wanted us to be ready for the larger world that would demand that we function biculturally.

Both my parents grew up in missionary schools established by evangelical Christians. Going to these schools was like winning the lottery in our community. Families who could afford to would send their kids to missionary schools not intending for the religious teaching to affect them but for access to an educational system that guaranteed a bright future. My parents experienced different outcomes of being in these institutions. My dad took what he needed to succeed in life and left the rest. He kept his Ethiopian Orthodox faith and his national pride. For him missionary school was a cultural experience and great academic opportunity.

My mother, on the other hand, has always been tender-hearted toward the Lord. She was raised Ethiopian Orthodox, but she was deeply affected by the Bible teaching of the missionary school she attended and missed it as an adult. She eventually left the Orthodox Church my parents were married in and joined an evangelical church. That changed the course of her life. She found the God she'd been searching for all her life. The gospel she was exposed to in her school had finally become clear and she was free to worship her king. As much as this freedom was a blessing to her soul, it came with a price in her day-to-day life. She was treated at times as a traitor to her forefathers' faith while interacting with friends and family. She was shamed for embracing what seemed like a foreign religion that everyone was afraid of. I watched her walk the fine line of loving and honoring her family while fully surrendering to Christ. It was what pulled me to Christ at an early age; to see a love like that toward people and God was otherworldly.

Missionary schools played a major role in creating tension between northern Ethiopia, which is majority Ethiopian Orthodox, and southern Ethiopia, which was historically not Christian and where missionaries settled heavily, creating a large evangelical movement. They also created tension within families like mine. Kids would be sent to these schools as Ethiopian Orthodox Christians looking for education but come out with "the white man's religion" as their own. This created problems with their families, because they no longer saw eye to eye with their loved ones.

This new way of exercising faith was not only culturally foreign but also a threat to the advancement of Ethiopian culture and ideologies because of the way it was intended to benefit society. For example, the Mennonite missionaries taught that women must wear long dresses and put on head coverings, which was in direct opposition to the growing independence movement of women at the time. Women who were educated and were looked on as the leaders of the next generation started wearing head coverings and chose to put their careers on hold to raise their children. That caused alarm to their families, who had sacrificed everything for these girls' education and future.

As a society, Ethiopia was actively trying to get out of poverty by educating as many men and women as possible to join the modern workforce. But these missionary practices seemed to pull the country backward, with educated women reverting to the lifestyles their parents had worked so hard to escape. Most of them came from families in rural areas, where a woman's traditional route to securing a better future was to marry a wealthy man. Education was the only way out, but this new path created isolation. Many women who found freedom in Christ also became culturally handicapped.

Watching that process unfold in my mother's life marked my childhood. I saw how a mission that had not been thoroughly contextualized could have a painful and destructive impact on the receiver. Not only that, but this type of movement always required a foreigner to be the leader, because the locals were ostracized and cast aside for stepping outside their culture. They were unable to be an effective witness in their Jerusalem. It was not the best strategy, nor did it include a deeply thorough discipleship process that allowed the born-again believer to go and disciple others. It was simply a culture war—and an ineffective strategy that caused unnecessary persecution and kept the gospel from spreading like wildfire.

Something else that marked my childhood was the unconditional love my mom showed my dad and her four children. She was a walking testimony of God's faithfulness and his steadfast love. Every morning I could count on being awakened by her prayer, hands on my forehead saying God's blessings over me. I knew I was seen, known, and loved by God. I had no fear of the enemy nor did I doubt God's protection over me. She would read his Word over us before going to bed whether we understood it at the time or not. She kept her covenant with the Lord, who has in turn pursued and captured our hearts as adults. The missionary we needed lived in our home.

Seeing my mother remain steadfast in her love and devotion to Christ despite the persecution she endured won my heart to Christ. The power of Christ exuded in her daily walk compelled me to follow him to a foreign land that would become my home. On December 26, 2003, a year after graduating from high school, I moved to the United States for college. I had identified a call to full-time ministry at age sixteen but that wasn't something I could pursue back home.

So I came to America with hopes of fulfilling the Great Commission in a place where I hoped to find many who shared my passion and zeal to reach the world with the truth of the gospel. I enrolled at a Christian college in Virginia, which became the place where I had the most beautiful spiritual and painful cultural awakenings. Although I didn't know it at the time, my journey as a Black evangelical Christian in America had started to unfold the moment my feet touched its soil. I was caught in a spiderweb of history that, as I started to untangle it, led me to see the parallels between injustices on the mission field and those voiced by Black and Brown Christians in white evangelical spaces.

The question remains: How do we fix it? I can tell you it will never be fixed until the Global South starts telling its own story. It is time for the lion to write, for us to tell our stories as they are and to find a path to truly heal and unify. In this way the story stops glorifying the hunter and starts giving glory to the Lamb of God who was slain for all humanity.

ONE

THE AWAKENING

We will never understand the significance of Jesus Christ
if we do not understand the rage he can provoke.

EUGENE PETERSON

MOVING TO THE UNITED STATES at the age of nineteen
had crucial racial implications for someone like me who grew
up sheltered and surrounded by role models who were all Black.
Although I was inundated by Western culture in Ethiopia, I
experienced it as an international introduction to prepare me
for the real world ruled by such a culture. My parents knew to
give me a leg up so I would have a fighting chance of surviving
a world ruled by Western influence. Part of that process was
making sure I spoke English and was familiar with American
culture, but that preparation failed to factor in my race. Where
I am from, people fully understand the economic disadvantage
of living in a developing country, but they don't consider their
race as a factor because everybody looks the same. In that
regard we were the majority living in a colorblind world.

In her book *Why Are All the Black Kids Sitting Together in the
Cafeteria?* Beverly Tatum details how microaggressions and

subtle racial profiling place a chip on the shoulders of Black and Brown American adolescents, who begin to develop a racial identity far earlier than their white peers. She writes, "As the result of a new and heightened awareness of the significance of race, the individual begins to grapple with what it means to be a member of a group targeted by racism. Research suggests that this focused process of examination of one's racial or ethnic identity may begin as early as middle or junior high school."[1] As an outsider I experienced this process later in life, while in college. Although it was delayed for me because I grew up in Ethiopia, it began as soon as my feet touched American soil.

I came expecting to experience a sense of discomfort until I was integrated into the new culture. For the first couple of years I was okay with that discomfort and I took my time being an outsider learning to become an insider. It's not like my new friends had any prior memory or experience of living a similar type of life as me, so I had no expectations of fitting in. I thought my peers were trying to figure me out as much as I was trying to figure them out. The racial problems became apparent once I got used to the culture and started working my way toward rightfully earning a spot in this new society I was now part of. I had done my part in speaking the language, winning scholarships, working on campus and appreciating the culture, even to the extent of understanding their humor. I knew once I started laughing with my friends while watching *Napoleon Dynamite* or *Elf* that I truly had arrived at a level of understanding the college culture I was a part of. I expected to eventually find a welcoming community that would extend hospitality, teach me its ways, and help me make this place my new home.

Unfortunately the natural progression of cultural integration didn't seem to work in my case. I benefited from the hospitality of a few wonderful friends, but they were the exception and not the rule. There were no open arms welcoming me to my global church family; I was invisible and my story irrelevant. My dream of linking up arm in arm to worship Jesus and reach the world together with the hope of his gospel remained a dream. My ultimate goal in coming to the United States was to eventually go back home to serve my people, so I was purposeful in learning Scripture and finding a community of believers that would rally behind me.

Even though there were subtle hints that told me true hospitality was out of the question for someone like me, I didn't have the framework to understand why. I was too naive and colorblind to associate the distance being placed between me and others who were white as a racial issue. On top of that, my immigration process and my studies kept me busy. Renewing visas every now and then to make sure I remained in good status while trying to keep my grades up and going through homesickness and loneliness all took on a life of their own. One thing I didn't have was time to sit down and contemplate the larger racial framework that was impacting my daily life.

I experienced uncomfortable but oddly similar interactions with my new friends and strangers alike. For example, the first time I was made aware that I was Black was when a man who hosted a church barbecue at his house approached me and asked, "Do you feel like you have an easier time being accepted in white circles as a Black woman because you are light-skinned?" You can imagine my shock as I had no idea what he was talking about. My cultural identity didn't have a race. It certainly had an ethnicity—Ethiopian—but not a race. I was flustered because I had many questions of my own but, most importantly, at that moment I was deeply hurt because I realized he did not see me as one of his own. No matter how much I loved Jesus, I was never going to be one of them. I felt unwelcome in his home and wanted to run back to my dorm.

Despite my pain and feeling of being blindsided, I had to find a respectful way to excuse myself from the conversation. The emotions that came after were new, anger and confusion that became sadness, which added to my homesickness. There was no one in that circle with whom I could have processed what I had just experienced. It was now my problem to deal with, even though it was this man who saw me differently and pointed it out. I had to carry the burden of his ignorance and deal with it, alone. This experience marked the beginning of the rest of my journey in white evangelical circles.

Jesus expects us to love even our enemies, but how do we love someone who wounds us so deeply and doesn't even know it? It is difficult to apply Scripture in this dynamic so the relationship can be restored: "If your brother sins against you, go tell him his fault, between you and him alone. If he listens to you, you have won your brother. But if he won't listen, take one or two others with you, so that by the testimony of two or three witnesses every fact may be established" (Matthew 18:15-16). I was invited into this man's home after entering his church and living in his country. There was no way I could express my grievance to someone with a visible advantage over me in every sense. I had to deal with it in my own way. I minimized the impact and kept looking for other circles where people might think differently. It's sad to think back and realize that it was only once I had endured the microaggressions that doors opened and allowed me to step into leadership and ministry roles. I guess I passed the test of being a "safe Black person" who wasn't going to be a troublemaker.

I forced myself to accept life in America as it was presented to me in my white evangelical spaces. It didn't take much time to learn that I needed to lean on my international friends for support and community, because they were going through similar situations based on their skin tone and where they were from. According to student mission organization The Traveling Team, there are almost a million international students in the United States each year. Sixty-two percent of these international students are from 10/40 Window countries—nearly half a million students. Eighty percent will return to their countries having never been invited to an American home. Forty percent of the world's heads of state have studied in the United States, but only 10 percent of international students are reached by US ministries.[2] Most, if not all, of my friends and I were already believers who chose to go to a Christian college, but our race was a roadblock preventing us from fully being part of the community that intentionally kept us at bay. So how would nonbelievers who need to be pursued, loved, invited in, and welcomed feel about their experience with American Christians?

We became each other's support system, and we came up with ways to answer questions from our white peers that we felt were intrusive, insensitive, or asked too frequently. We needed quick and witty responses that would satisfy their curiosity so they would leave us alone. It was clear to us that their questions were not meant to get closer to us but about research. For example, my top three most-asked questions were, "What's Ethiopia like?" "Were you a Christian before coming to the United States?" and "Can I touch your hair?" My answers were: "It's home," "Ethiopia is one of the oldest Christian nations in the world," and "*No.*" Someone once had the audacity to ask a Kenyan friend if she had seen a car before coming here. She responded sarcastically, "No, I rode lions to school." The idea of being from a country in Africa somehow made us primitive to them and shaped how our peers saw us. It hindered their ability to extend a dignified question that would be a bridge to building a relationship. It was obvious that while we were crossculturally trained from a young age to not only function but lead in Western culture, our white peers were not even aware of their own culture. Our interaction was not harmonious; in fact it was frustrating to have to be the object of their crosscultural training when their parents and churches should have done that for them.

These people, who believed they were called to be missionaries to our countries, could not even have a simple conversation with us as their peers. We were extensions of our people; therefore we were probably put in place by God to help them learn and grow while in the comfort of their home. Their training for missions focused on finding primitive people somewhere around the world and saving them, so they didn't have the lens to see how building a friendship with Black and Brown people in their communities was the first step to building a bridge to the larger work God was calling them to. Seeing this missed opportunity, it was natural for us to wonder why they were being sent to our people. How would they be called to the nations when they couldn't even be friends with their neighbors? For my part, I wanted to do everything I could to mitigate the issue of white saviorism on the mission field so my people would not be exposed to such ignorance.

I found some relief from the condescending culture when I moved to the DC area after college. The Lord opened an internship opportunity at a megachurch, which became my home. It was a place where I was mentored and discipled by some of the most dynamic leaders who loved God and honored his name. My particular campus was very diverse. It had no single ethnic group that could be considered a majority. I imagine heaven is like that, with everyone equally represented. It was in that place that I started to feel normal again and to understand that true multiethnic churches can exist. I saw men and women from all ethnicities and walks of life choosing to follow Jesus. It was spiritually vibrant and physically colorful. It was a place of rest, healing, and restoration. Learning how to minister to people who were different from me prepared me for what was to come in my future ministry career. And it gave me a desire to see true multiethnic churches that will set the stage for the global mission movement and beautiful mutuality.

FINDING A NEW COMMUNITY

In September of 2016, while my husband and I were in the process of moving to Charlotte, North Carolina, news broke about the shooting of Keith Lamont Scott by a police officer.

The Queen City's streets filled with mourners lamenting Scott's death and protesting for justice. At the time I had just started to develop a deeper understanding of the framework of racism and how it had shaped America. Since this was happening so close to my new home, it forced me to open my eyes and confront realities that had real implications for my family. As the wife of a Black man and mother of a Black child, I needed to understand what it meant for us to live in the South and how my faith plays a role in this intersection.

As I look back today on our move, I see that it was not a coincidence that I was introduced to Charlotte during a public outcry for justice. I had just been invited to join a Christ-centered racial reconciliation Facebook group called Be the Bridge by a friend who had adopted her kids from Ethiopia and was starting to wrestle with their experience of being Black in America. As I watched her grow in her role as a white parent who was engaged in their cultural struggles, I was impressed by her cultural awareness. It was encouraging to see the work she was doing on herself so her kids wouldn't have to be her educators. I rarely saw this type of dedication in other white friends, so I jumped into this group to see what type of environment had given her such sensitivity to her kids' cultural experience.

That environment quickly became the place where I began to awaken to my own blindness to racial injustice and inequalities all around me. Living half my life surrounded by people who looked and talked like me had given me the experience of the majority culture; therefore I had a lot of listening to do to Black and Brown voices with minority experiences.

Listening to them gave me the language I needed to voice my own experience and tell my story in a culture that no longer centers my experience. Once I learned the implications of systemic racism, I understood that as the larger racial problem people of color deal with every day in America. I realized I was not constantly running into unkind or ignorant white people, nor were they reacting to something I had done; they, too, were taught to see me differently. What a deeply strategized spiritual warfare that has plagued the church for centuries and prevented her from experiencing true community! Yet no one was talking about the spiritual implications of racism, giving the enemy further power to divide us.

While I was in the midst of this awakening, Scott's death was the backdrop against which I finally pieced together an understanding of the systemic racism America was built around. The protesters of his death on the screen of my TV were not a distant annoyance or a disconnected group to which I got to assign a biased narrative in my head. They were my brothers and sisters, my new neighbors and descendants of my people. These were the people who fought for equality and freedom so I could proudly declare myself a Black immigrant woman and walk with my head held high. They were people who continued to fight for their rights and had not chosen cruel retaliation as payment for what they had endured for generations. These were the descendants of strong and powerful men and women who had not only survived but continued to excel against all odds. This time around, those faces on the screen were kin to me and I had nothing but compassion. I finally understood what Dr. King meant when he said, "A riot is the language of the unheard."

When things calmed down in the city, the talk of racial reconciliation died down in our new church, and it seemed to be completely forgotten within six months or so. In my online community full of Black and Brown people, however, the issues never died. We faced them every day, sharing prayer requests about how to teach our children about racism without destroying their innocence. We discussed how to lovingly confront coworkers about their racist behavior. Trying to apply Matthew 18 to this dynamic seemed impossible, since the white evangelical spaces we found ourselves in don't recognize racism as a corporate or individual sin needing to be addressed biblically. We had to sit with the sorrow of these realizations and lick our own wounds without community. A dear friend Karen, who recognized the need, assembled female ministry leaders working in white spaces and created a support group for us, a collective for women of color that helped us find the encouragement our churches and parachurch ministries were not able to give. She said, "We are the Brown faces in white spaces that God has placed to do his work of reconciliation, and that is our mission field."

AWAKE AND ON MISSION

Although the city of Charlotte was racially divided, my church was heavily involved in annual short-term mission trips to Haiti and the Dominican Republic. By then I had made the decision not to participate in any missional activities that didn't start from their own neighborhoods. Every time an invitation to go on one of these short-term trips was extended to me, I found myself tensing up, wondering how in the world this made sense to my fellow church family. Our city was still

20

wounded from communal trauma and Black people were still trying to heal, but instead of pouring our resources into restoring trust and praying for healing, we were making a tone-deaf move: mobilizing white people to go reach Black people in a faraway land. I suspected perhaps this was a subconscious effort to ease the guilt and discomfort racism brought up in our church folks. It broke my heart that the remedy for the privileged was to go to another Black community to make themselves feel better while they ignored the needs nearby.

As a person of the Black diaspora who is part of both the Black community in America and the Black global community, I don't agree with such a mission. I feel like I have been given a front-row seat to watch how a system that builds up one group of people and suppresses another continues to run without hindrance because we insist on being colorblind. A church that turns a blind eye to her neighbors but travels around the world to feed the "poor" is not only hypocritical but actively hurting the Great Commission:

> Jesus came near and said to them, "All authority has been given to me in heaven and on earth. Go, therefore, and make disciples of all nations, baptizing them in the name of the Father and of the Son and of the Holy Spirit, teaching them to observe everything I have commanded you. And remember, I am with you always, to the end of the age." (Matthew 28:18-20)

The Great Commission was given to disciples who knew Christ and gave up everything to follow him. It was given to those who had experienced a life-altering faith, one they were eager to share with the world. The life they lived with Christ compelled them to speak to everyone they encountered so that they became carriers of the gospel around the world. How can there be a mission movement without such disciples? Jesus didn't mince words; he wants those who go to be his true followers, not hug givers or housepainters. This means that as much as we're eager to fulfill the Great Commission, we must first start with the great commandment—loving our neighbor as ourselves.

One of the best things I've seen and learned from ten plus years of ministry in majority culture churches is the careful attention given to local discipleship. I've been a part of small group ministry movements that transform church culture in evangelical spaces. I have learned a great deal about the meticulous processes and checks and balances designed to help churches avoid placing people in leadership who are harboring or vulnerable to moral failure. The selection process for these leaders is deliberate and detailed, and as a result it is difficult to find an unqualified person leading. We have created intricate applications and scrupulous interview strategies to help us select leaders who will care for the spiritual well-being of the body, while preparing ongoing trainings and coaching to help them grow. There are teams that write curricula and create tactics to make small groups something people want to be a part of. I have acquired a great deal of knowledge and confidence in choosing whose leadership I submit to in my personal spiritual journey because of what I have seen done right in these places. If there is a topic I can talk about for days, it is how many guardrails healthy churches have placed around their processes as safeguards from failure. But when it comes to selecting and preparing individuals to do the very thing Jesus commanded his church to do before ascending into heaven, integrity is lacking.

What continues to floor me is the lack of connection between all these values and processes and the mission movement. I have not seen any of the leadership models we use to develop our small group leaders locally or any of the processes designed to ensure accountability in our local congregations being carried over as we send people off to other countries to "lead." I have seen these responsibilities handed off to parachurch ministries when it comes to sending long-term missionaries, but they're completely overlooked in short-term missions. This neglect results from a lack of knowledge as well as biased assumptions that the ends justify the means. These practices give churches permission to send people they have no business sending at the expense of the receiver.

As I noticed the church's failure to uphold standards of leadership and accountability on the mission field, it occurred to me that it was catering to the needs of its consumers—the goers. Who was looking out for the receivers who would be consumed by these unhealthy practices? It made me wonder what would motivate people to go to a place or a people group they didn't value. Did they know what the impact of their good intentions would be?

If we truly loved God's global church, we would not give her our bare minimum or send underqualified workers for the sake of their "experience." We would send people who saw her people as image bearers of the king and had hearts of servant leaders, wanting to wash the feet of the people to whom they were called. Instead, what we see in these mission trips is a desire to center oneself and exploit the other. The individualistic nature of the Western church is a byproduct of secular culture, and as a result it has failed to fulfill the call to make disciples of all nations.

This practice continues when white saviorism is the vehicle used to make an emotional appeal and recruit "missionaries" to go instead of equipping disciples to become witnesses wherever they are. Race and socioeconomic status are used as the number-one method for recruiting workers. Appeals such as this excerpt from a 2017 article are very common:

> Africa was once known as the "white man's graveyard." In the early days of the modern missionary movement, wave after wave of pioneer missionaries landed on the shores of this continent determined to establish a beachhead for the gospel of Jesus Christ. These early men and women laid down their lives to disease and a hostile population for the sake of the gospel. As historian Ruth Tucker notes, "Africa has claimed the lives of more . . . missionaries than any other area of the world." Yet still they came. It was these 19th-century missionary pioneers, Tucker writes, "who risked all to open the way for Christianity in Africa."
>
> Today there are cures for diseases like malaria and dysentery, and many indigenous peoples in Africa have joined the urbanization migration. Still, the challenge facing our generation to bring the gospel to every corner of the continent is no less daunting than it was 200 years ago.[3]

This is a perfectly crafted appeal to white saviorism, informed by a racist and colonial picture of mission. What's rarely seen is the other perspective. If we rewrote this appeal to read as follows, we'd see how divided the global mission movement is:

> Colonialism is known as "the Black man's graveyard." After white people stepped foot on the beautiful continent of Africa, death and desolation followed. Many families were ripped apart, little boys and girls stolen from their homes and sold off into slavery in a faraway land. While treated in the most inhumane conditions, they had to begin a life of enslavement away from the land where God created them to be free and to possess. The white man has claimed more African lives than any other race in the world and has done so in the name of Jesus Christ.

As shocking and even offensive as this might sound, it is just a hint of how my people see Western mission. The difference between what Africans think the white man has done to them and what the white man thinks he's done for them is like night and day. It's why we need to explore this topic further.

If white churches continue using racial and emotional appeals to mobilize their people, the response will be a racial and emotional resistance to their efforts. We do in fact reap what we sow, and the time has come to pause and reflect on the methods being used to do mission. Although the white savior version of mission might resonate with white people, it is met with resistance by people of color, who have always struggled with the version of Western mission that dehumanized their ancestors. The claim that the white man opened the door to African Christianity in the nineteenth century is untrue, as African Christianity dates all the way back to the first century. As the BBC's *Story of Africa* series states, "The Christian communities in North Africa were among the earliest in the world."[4] Just because the white man got to participate in the nineteenth century doesn't mean we have to rewrite our history.

This is something too important to ignore, something that is damaging the name of Christ and the work of the gospel throughout the global church. Unless we confront the elephant in the room that's standing in the way of us seeing each other as equals, we cannot work together. Western Christians who have the power and means to inflict pain and walk away without immediate repercussion have little awareness of the magnitude of their negative impact on the global church and the work of the Great Commission. Scripture is clear that God has given every part of his body an essential role in building his kingdom. In 1 Corinthians 12:

> But as it is, God has arranged each one of the parts in the body just as he wanted. And if they were all the same part, where would the body be? As it is, there are many parts, but one body. The eye cannot say to the hand, "I don't need you!" Or again, the head can't say to the feet, "I don't need you!" On the contrary, those parts of the body that are weaker are indispensable. And those parts of the body that we consider less honorable, we clothe these with greater honor, and our unrespectable parts are treated with greater respect, which our respectable parts do not need. (1 Corinthians 12:18-24)

The cultural superiority of the West has inflicted a one-sided mission movement on the rest of the world, demanding that all cultures embrace and elevate their superior approach to theology and godliness as their own. How can we be united in our efforts to reach the lost when we are lost ourselves?

The need to intersect justice with the mission movement is undeniably central to the gospel because of how valuable Jesus made it to be. He always saw and addressed the social conditions of people, and by doing so he revealed his power to them. When it comes to any social issue other than racism, Western Christianity actively uses social justice as a catalyst and a strategy to do mission work effectively. For example, it has helped rescue women from sex trafficking and organized conferences around that particular issue of injustice. This response is necessary, but it misses the mark when it leaves out one of the central injustices in the world: racism. Whether it's been the inflicter of injustice or played a role of the "savior," Western Christianity has always had a part in social justice. Therefore it's incumbent on leaders of the modern mission movement to pay attention to the racial injustices that have infiltrated the Western church and have been packaged and sent out with their missionaries. As fish don't know when they're in water, most mission organizations are unaware of the cultural burden they impose on indigenous leaders when they demand their way as the best to reach a people group that has graciously invited them in. Keeping the autonomy of the culture gives indigenous leaders a wider reach, therefore Western leaders must pull back and do some work to gain the self-awareness required to pursue justice for the kingdom. When they do that, they make a way for the gospel to be preached in all cultures, languages, and tongues freely. This is the only way it can spread like wildfire without the hindrance of modern-day colonialism that demands conformity to white culture. Being awake to racism only creates a greater awareness to the restoration work that awaits God's people in the global mission movement. And that's exactly what the church of Christ needs to lead with.

TWO

THE MISSIONARY

*But you will receive power when the Holy Spirit has
come on you, and you will be my witnesses in Jerusalem,
in all Judea and Samaria, and to the ends of the earth.*

ACTS 1:8

THE WAY I'VE GROWN UP to understand the term *mis-sionary* was typically referring to someone who lives cross-culturally long-term. In the Western mission movement, missionaries are typically identified by their affiliations to a philanthropic work and rarely by their character.

I've always struggled with the term *missionary*. First, I haven't seen people who look like me bearing that name as an indication of their dedication to Christ. Second, the term doesn't translate into my language without the association of a foreign concept of practicing Christianity in a way that doesn't lend itself to my culture. The word has always felt like a term ascribed to good white people at best and colonial at worst, not biblical. In Ethiopia, when we use that term we explicitly mean a foreigner who practices faith-based humanitarianism. Today the meaning of the term is starting to shift a bit, but while I was growing up, I met hardly any "missionaries" in the sense Western culture understands them who weren't white. We refer to our local missionaries as *wongelawi/t* (singular male/female). This term describes being sent by God for the work of the gospel; it literally means "gospel carrier" or "evangelist." The *wongelawian* (plural) I grew up admiring were known for their Christlike character rather than the type of work they did, so the term *missionary* seemed to abandon that for me. I struggled with the term and its implications of being a doer of good more than a carrier of the good news. As a believer who left home for the sake of the gospel, there came a time when I needed to figure out if this term I struggled with the most—*missionary*—was a biblical term. As foreign as it was to me, I knew I must learn to accept it if it was something the Lord had called me to do, but if it wasn't, I wanted to be free from it.

BEING SENT

The word *mission* is not found in the Bible. It comes from the Latin word *missio*, which means "to send." The word *sent* is present at least eight hundred times in the Old Testament and several times in the New Testament. God sends not only his people but also himself throughout the Bible, which includes the ultimate sending of his one and only Son, Jesus Christ, to be a sacrifice for humanity. Scripture is clear that when God sends his people, he sends them to do his work in his name and not to make a name for themselves. Being sent by God is costly as seen throughout the Bible. *Šālaḥ*, which is Hebrew for being "sent," is used to describe Moses in Exodus:

But Moses asked God, "Who am I that I should go to Pharaoh and that I should bring the Israelites out of Egypt?"

He answered, "I will certainly be with you, and this will be the sign to you that I am the one who sent you: when you bring the people out of Egypt, you will all worship God at this mountain." (Exodus 3:11-12)

Faithful ones are seen all over Scripture. Abraham, who was called by God away from everything he knew to a life of full surrender, saw a vision and believed in a calling that kept God's purpose front and center. Joseph, who was forced into a life of slavery and imprisonment in a foreign land, rose as a wise leader who saved not only Egypt but Israel as well and fulfilled the dream God gave him at a young age. Ruth, who chose to follow the God of her mother-in-law and ended up in the genealogy of Jesus, responded to God's call to follow him wherever he would send her. Daniel, who was exiled and put into a lion's den because of his faith, came out alive bearing witness of the greatness of God. God has written the stories of faithful believers who obediently left or were forced out of their homes to pursue their God-given calling and by grandiose measures made his name known. These immigrants and refugees followed God through many trials and persecutions, but they remained faithful to his mission. Today American churches have a growing tension with the immigrant community, much less consider them as missionaries. Yet God continues to do his work in the lives of those who have accepted the call to go to reach their hosts.

As I've become more fully aware of God's mission through my immigration journey, I've started to embrace my story. It is a story of God's pursuit of my heart as I traveled the hard paths before me and continued to choose him, those choices becoming a witness to those around me. It is the story of a visible, engaged, and tangible God in my life, without whom I would not be where I am today. God used my difficult road to give me access to people I would have never been able to meet or know. I didn't have to go seek the "unreached groups" in order to share the good news, nor did I have to pray for God to give me a heart for the nations. He brought me to the nations and took me through one of the most difficult journeys so I can identify with the suffering of many. During those times, I would have never dared to say I was a missionary. I didn't have a sending agency that represented me, I was not reporting to anyone except God. Nor was I being financially supported and emotionally encouraged by a body of Christ. I was alone, a Black immigrant Christian girl, who had no cultural or physical proximity to the word *missionary*. Finding and being exposed to the works of people like Dr. Sam George from the Lausanne Movement, which point us to God's wonderful work in the diaspora community, have emboldened me to dare and view my journey as one of a missionary. The term I had resisted using to describe myself has now become a term I'd use boldly, because I've come to realize no one except God through the Holy Spirit can give me this title.

I now understand that a missionary is one who makes a choice to pick up the cross and follow Christ on a daily basis. It is a call of deep and costly discipleship that enables us to live a life God has intended for the Christian to live. That is when we will experience a joy so deep it's immovable by circumstances around us. The meaning of true comfort that comes from belonging to a community of believers who love one another sacrificially becomes apparent to the faithful missionary. The missionary's journey is marked by being known, pursued, loved, and used by God. It is a life lived on the edge of the unknown but completely rested on the One who calls us. That call produces a character that's attractive to the lost soul who is seeking meaning and purpose. Of course we need all the tools Western mission has afforded us—Bible translation in each language and meeting physical and financial needs are wonderful—but these tools should not be confused with the call of becoming a mature believer, a person of character, and a gospel carrier.

THE POWER OF CHARACTER

Mission work as seen in the Bible is not an institutionalized practice nor is it a profession one chooses but a life to which all believers are called. In the Gospels, we observe the followers of Christ being given an opportunity to factor in the danger of being sent by God when they counted the cost of following Jesus at the beginning of their journey as his disciples. That's the very reason baptisms were such a big deal, they were signs of dying to self, abandoning the world and its fruits to a new life of sacrifice for the gospel. Today, many question evangelicalism because it seems to center itself around comfort and worldly success and has abandoned reflecting the character of Jesus to the world. Some leave the faith and others seriously and justifiably distance themselves from the church because they don't find in it the type of faithful Christianity displayed in the Bible by the disciples. There is a great opportunity for we who call ourselves followers of Jesus to become witnesses to the world around us by going back to our calling to be missionaries. Inviting people to church is no longer a viable option or tool of evangelism. No longer do people get excited by churches with bright lights and great worship music; they can go to a better-lit and more exciting concert. They have daily pressing reasons to question our faith and our affiliations, and we must truly step into our divine calling, becoming carriers of the gospel of Jesus Christ.

As our character is in question more than ever, our churches have a beautiful opportunity to teach and disciple believers about a robust faith that centers around building a global body of believers who are multiethnic. Yet we must exercise great caution because the Western mission movement is associated with colonialism. Especially because it tends to use language such as, "We are going to go into the world to plant Jesus flags." This type of language has a colonial and oppressive tone that further creates distance between us (the Global South) and them (Westerners). The world is desperate for Jesus, but it's not desperate for white saviorism; therefore it is on Western Christians to divorce their faith from imperialism. History has taught those of us from the Global South that we need to move with great caution when it comes to Western ideologies. There is a great need for building trust with communities that have been historically harmed by Western politics, religion, and ideologies, and we shouldn't be surprised when we're met by resistance to the institutionalized mission strategy of others. No amount of funding and strategy can rewrite the past and create reconciliation. Yet there are no bridges that cannot be built or crossed with the Spirit of God, who leads us to repentance.

A closer look at Acts 1:8 shows us the clear instruction and swift strategy Jesus gives to his disciples for making an impact around the world. It's a simple and powerful yet heavily overlooked model in Western Christianity. The church was birthed on Pentecost when the Holy Spirit filled the disciples with power and sent them on mission. Before that moment, they had been waiting diligently in prayer and community because they knew going without the Holy Spirit was fruitless. Their character was developed during their time with Jesus and after his death and resurrection in their waiting. These disciples stood up for the rights of the oppressed and continued to heal and teach people just as Jesus had taught them to do.

Being in worship of Christ and in ministry in the United States, I have observed a false dichotomy in Western mission movements, one that emphasizes going somewhere far away without first making sure those going have a lifestyle that resembles Christ. There was a major difference between the twelve disciples who lived with Christ and everyone else who followed him. Jesus entrusted the mission to the few and sent them—not the masses. They knew the Messiah closely and had received the Holy Spirit, who gave them strength to persevere through persecution. Western missiology solely focuses on Matthew 28:18-20, "All authority has been given to me. . . . Go, therefore . . . teaching them to observe everything I have commanded you." This makes Western Christians believe that their role in sharing the gospel starts when they go somewhere around the world, not when they accept Christ as their Savior. I have seen greater emphasis on "stay until you're filled with power" than on "go and make disciples" in other cultures who cling on to the power of the Holy Spirit for their ability to be a missionary. There is in Western theology a lack of emphasis on prayer, fasting, and the teaching of Christian persecution and identifying with Christ in our suffering; therefore we don't see the fruit of long-suffering in believers. This robs the church of the ability to not only send but even have faithful Christians who can do gospel work where they are. An emphasis to "BE" a disciple before "MAKING" disciples is necessary if the Western church is to remain an essential part of the global mission movement.

The power of a believer's testimony is the ultimate weapon of destruction against the enemy. As seen in Revelation 12:11:

> They conquered him
> by the blood of the Lamb
> and by the word of their testimony;
> for they did not love their lives
> to the point of death.

As believers who are called to carry the gospel around the world, our ability to testify of God's goodness in our lives has far more power than our ability to indoctrinate others.

Greg Ogden uses the acronym FAT, which stands for faithful, available, and teachable, to describe the people Jesus invested in and sent off as disciple makers.[1] Ogden also incorporates this tool and describes making disciples a few at a time in his book *Transforming Discipleship*, emphasizing character and willingness as deciding factors in whether time and energy should be invested in teaching someone to become a disciple maker.[2] This is ultimately the call to the mission field. We must ask ourselves, "What type of testimony do we have as believers that is worthy of spreading to the ends of the earth?" The mission is not an expedition, nor is it a story of us saving others. It is a call to die to self and live for Christ. It is sacrificial, it is costly, it is brutal, and it truly is a call to lose our presupposed identity so we can be one with Christ. Our life is to be eclipsed by his all-consuming fire that unites us with everything he is so that we are sure examples of Christ when the world interacts with us.

FAITHFUL LEGACY

There are many faithful Western missionaries whose stories have served as an encouragement to mine. George Müller, who was used massively by God to reach the orphans of Bristol is one of them.[3] When I thought that God required a faith like that to do his work in my life, I prayed that he would give me a testimony like Müller. I've mulled over how a woman like Gladys Aylward dared to step out in faith and go around the world to spread the love of Jesus Christ.[4] Aylward not only preached the love of Christ through her service in China as a "foot inspector" but also made room for the orphans in the community. These testimonies don't escape me, nor do I challenge modern Western missiology and practices because I want to rewrite history.

However, what stands out to me when I read their stories is how much these people loved God and did whatever he required of them, and often they suffered for it. That suffering was the main vehicle to their maturing in faith and what allowed them to see and identify others' pain. When we're wrapped around with comfort it's easy to turn a blind eye to another's pain, but when we, too, are suffering, something in us wants to prevent others' suffering because we know they don't deserve it. Christ suffered on our behalf so he could take away our pain, and there is a beauty in our ability to suffer with others—we get to honor the king and be close to him: "Consider it a great joy, my brothers and sisters, whenever you experience various trials, because you know that the testing of your faith produces endurance. And let endurance have its full effect, so that you may be mature and complete, lacking nothing" (James 1:2-4).

Looking at the lives of these missionaries we view as heroes, we see that they didn't start practicing sacrificial living once they got to a destination but were faithfully serving the Lord at home in their communities. In fact, some were pushed out or persecuted by the institutions they belonged to. One of those women is Margaret E. Barber, a British missionary to China who would eventually disciple one of the greatest faith leaders of China, Watchman Nee. Nee's teachings have probably influenced African and Asian theology more than any Western theologian, and Nee is a testament to God's work in accomplishing his mission by using anyone from any part of the world.

I had an opportunity to interview Dr. Grace May, associate professor of biblical studies and director of the Women's Institute at William Carey International University, about her dissertation, "Watchman Nee and the Breaking of Bread: The Missiological and Spiritual Forces that Contributed to an Indigenous Chinese Ecclesiology." She describes Nee as a man with high regard for community, worship, and Communion. His discipleship journey as nurtured by Barber led him to become one of the most influential theologians in the world. The irony is that once he became well-versed in Scripture, this brilliant teenage theologian confronted his teacher about her role as a woman teaching over men. Barber decided it was time for her to transfer her teaching role to Nee and allowed him to lead. She was an Anglican missionary in the nineteenth century who faithfully taught the theology she believed in without abandoning the parts that would be a disadvantage to her. Dr. May said to me, "Although we may not agree with or like the theology, we must pay attention to the character of Margaret to transfer power to a teenager to teach over her and for her to sit and listen to her student teach on her behalf." What a beautiful character of a disciple maker. At the end of the day the gospel may cost us something we hold on to tightly, something of comfort or a position of power. Are we faithful enough to submit to it?

There is something attractive about the lives of these missionaries who experienced the power of God through prayer and devotion. They did not have money or access to the latest mobilization strategies; they simply were faithful, teachable, and available. I'm not saying our modern attempt to mobilize young leaders is a bad thing, but I do want to challenge the model. Mobilization should take place around a biblical model of mission that demands their whole devotion and sacrifice of self for the gospel. The strategy Jesus imparted, which is to be filled with the Spirit and become a witness, is not complicated, nor does it break the bank for anyone. Yet we pour financial resources into building an institutionalized gospel that elevates feeding the physical body over the spiritual one. While we focus on meeting physical needs of the poor and recruiting missionaries who are capable of raising their annual salaries, we forget those around us with developed character, who could be key assets in reaching the world with the gospel.

Jesus didn't die on the cross and rise from the dead for the sake of bread and water. In fact, he said, "Man must not live on bread alone but on every word that comes from the mouth of God" (Matthew 4:4). The Western mission movement has somehow shifted its focus from sending those who can bear a witness of the resurrected Christ to those who can buy their own legacy through philanthropic effort. It undervalues sacrificial living and overvalues physical comfort, putting an institutional agenda before God's. We cannot expect to revolutionize the world with the message of the gospel when we're exporting prosperity gospel in our methods of sending. Our institutions are overcrowded with bureaucracy, which unfortunately leads to a legacy of self and not of Christ. This legacy is transactional, actively exploiting people inside and outside institutions at the cost of God's image bearers.

CONNECT THE DOTS

In most of our churches there is a disconnect between the mission (outreach) and discipleship departments. They operate as separate entities, which has produced in congregants a view of mission that divorces the gospel from its social implications. We have to work to bridge the gap and make mission an outworking of our faith. Discipleship is not just about studying the Bible in small groups, while mission is not just about going out to feed the poor. They are exclusively intertwined. We must push people out of their comfortable "discipleship" groups and challenge them to go wherever Jesus asks them to go, because discipleship is all-encompassing. Our churches are so busy planning outreach events that require us to go into "underserved communities" that they've forgotten to teach us to invite strangers into our homes. How does our going around the world benefit the kingdom when we've become so comfortable shutting the door in the faces of those God sends for us to receive? Where are the people who don't look like us, pray like us, vote like us, or act like us? When we become a witness to the gospel, we become hosts of strangers and escape becoming a lit lamp covered in a basket and sitting under a bed (Luke 8:16).

Jesus taught his disciples the truth of the gospel while also sending them out to do his work. For the disciples, there was no room for compartmentalization of faith; they in fact fed the hungry, healed the sick, and freed the oppressed while they prayed and testified of the Messiah in their living rooms. Signs and wonders followed them wherever they went—they were like a city on a hill. As believers our responsibility is to always go where there is darkness, not to sit comfortably where we're not necessarily needed. Our witness needs to move us from under our beds and into our Jerusalem, Judea, Samaria, and end of the world.

One of my favorite stories of the Bible is the interaction of Philip and the Ethiopian eunuch in Acts 8, which beautifully describes our role and God's role in missions. In the preceding chapters of Acts we see the apostles sharing the gospel in Jerusalem, with many coming to know Christ and being baptized by water and the Holy Spirit. The rapid growth in believers causes Saul to intensify his persecution of the church, which leads to Stephen's death by stoning and creates chaos among the believers.

Philip moves out to Samaria because of this persecution in Jerusalem and ends up sharing the gospel with Simon and his family, who are baptized. Then the Lord instructs Philip to go south of Jerusalem toward Gaza, where he meets the Ethiopian eunuch. The significance of how they meet is one we must not overlook. This man is the treasurer of Queen Candace's wealth and has a copy of the book of Isaiah, which makes him a very wealthy man. He is comfortably sitting on his chariot reading from Isaiah out loud when Philip approaches. Upon the instruction of the Holy Spirit to go join this man on the chariot, Philip obeys with a curiosity that is beautiful to see. He asks, "Do you understand what you're reading?" The man answers, "How can I . . . unless someone guides me?" (Acts 8:30-31). Philip doesn't insert himself in this man's life, although he could have. He chooses to lead with a question, which opens up the eunuch to a conversation. The eunuch invites Philip in, to help him understand God's Word clearly.

God by general revelation has revealed himself to everyone so that no one is without excuse (Romans 1:20). We have to be able to connect the dots by asking questions rather than leading with our assumptions. Philip approaches the man with curiosity, which honors him as an image bearer of God and acknowledges him as someone God has been pursuing from long before his meeting with Philip. What's surprising to me is that the eunuch had the awareness that he needed someone to guide him through the scroll's contents. Because God had been preparing his heart to hear the good news, he was in a way waiting for Philip. Not only does Philip get to share the gospel with the Ethiopian eunuch, he also gets to baptize him. This baptism also surprisingly happens at the request of the eunuch, who sees a river and says, "Look, there's water. What would keep me from being baptized?" (Acts 8:36).

This beautiful interaction between these two men not only shows Philip's calling to share the gospel but also God's previous work in the recipient's heart and continuing work after the gospel is shared with him. As God was preparing the eunuch's heart to receive the gospel, he also directed him to be baptized. We don't typically hear that in our pulpits; the Western way of looking at this story typically centers Philip's calling or even heroism and neglects to identify God's work in the eunuch's life prior to Philip and after him. Scripture is full of stories about God's work in people's hearts all around the world and the obedience of a few faithful followers being used as messengers of the good news as they flee persecution of all kinds. If we identify as faithful, available, and teachable servants, we must understand that our comfort, satisfaction, or legacy was never part of our calling. Yet the honor we receive as we identify with Christ in suffering is our reward. The sanctification that comes with being used as his vessels to reach his children all around the world is what makes this missionary journey unique and not for the masses.

God fulfills his role and prepares the hearts of the people he will send us to. Our role is to keep in step with the Spirit and obey when he calls us. Once we meet those whose hearts we believe have been prepared, we must lead with questions rather than assumptions. Like Philip, we must be available to anyone who might need us. Philip, a Jewish man, was asked a question by a Gentile, but he was humble, ready, and effective. This interaction not only had a spiritual but a cultural component to it, as well. We don't see Philip trying to put down a man he might believe to be unclean or use his position to exploit him to improve his own comfort and status. Philip took every opportunity and used it to do the work God called him to do, but, most beautifully, he left when he was no longer needed. In fact the Spirit of the Lord carried Philip away. I believe this was because the eunuch had everything he needed to carry the gospel with him to his people. God saw fit to send Philip elsewhere. My hope is that our churches produce missionaries like Philip, who go where God calls them, who say yes to the things that are asked of them, who share with curiosity to learn about where people are with God and figure out their role, and who have no agenda to convert people so they can conquer their lands and dominate their culture.

When we emphasize going on mission as the ultimate calling without exposing people to ways of becoming true missionaries, we build institutionalized religion. But when we emphasize faithfulness, availability, and teachability, we empower each individual believer to take up their cross and carry it to wherever the Lord calls them. Just as the disciples were emboldened after the Holy Spirit came upon them, our character is what glorifies Christ when we serve him from a place of becoming one with him. The disciples didn't leave Jerusalem because they "felt called" to Judea, Samaria, and the end of the world. Even though Jesus had instructed them to go, they were pushed out of Jerusalem because of the offensiveness of their gospel message to the Pharisees. They rocked the political power and confronted the sin of religious leaders, which endangered their lives to the point they had to flee. A massacre targeting Christians at the instruction of Saul (later Paul) caused a massive exodus, releasing immigrants and refugees to reach the world with the message of the gospel.

Although our struggles may not be as dramatic as the apostles', we are still called to a kingdom that demands the same dedication the disciples displayed. Our journey of pursuing Christ, although not glamorous, produces fruit that honors his creation and attracts those whose hearts beat to meet their Creator. Our calling is to be an aroma of Christ wherever he may call us and for that aroma to be so strong that it reaches the whole world around us. It is a worthy call to disciple a few faithful people in our living rooms, to pray for the martyrs of the faith around the globe, and to go when called on by God himself—not because of a spiritually manipulative sermon that generates guilt for our comfortable lifestyle. The mission is not a Western Christian's effort to prove to the world that they are good people who give out of their surplus. It's a call to tell the world the good news of Jesus Christ, even if it costs our lives.

Therefore let us pull back our efforts to go reach the world and focus on investing in the lives of believers by making disciples who have transformed lives. May our churches produce true missionaries that are witnesses of the gospel by the power of their character and witness to those around them, missionaries who have counted the cost, live in submission to the spirit, and reject worldly conformity by standing for peace, justice, and reconciliation on behalf of those on the margins.

THREE

THE DOCTRINE OF DISCOVERY

This hand is not the color of yours, but if I pierce it, I shall feel pain. If you pierce your hand, you also feel pain. The blood that will flow from mine will be of the same color as yours. I am a man. The same God made us both.

PONCA CHIEF STANDING BEAR

IN NOVEMBER 2018, we watched in horror as John Chau, a twenty-six-year-old American adventure blogger and evangelical missionary, was killed by the isolated tribe he was attempting to convert to Christianity. Even though the evangelical mission organization that trained him hailed him as a martyr, his family and friends were saddened by the misguided beliefs that led to his death. They said, "Chau's decision to contact the Sentinelese, who have made it clear over the years that they prefer to be left alone, was indefensibly reckless. But it was not a spontaneous act of recklessness by a dimwitted thrill-seeker; it was a premeditated act of recklessness by a fairly intelligent and thoughtful thrill-seeker who spent years preparing, understood the risks, including to his own life, and believed his purpose on earth was to bring Christ to the island he considered 'Satan's last stronghold.'"[1]

As much as this story evokes empathy for Chau's family, it also brings to light the attempt to invade and convert as one of the main tools used in "reaching the unreached." The assumption that this place was Satan's stronghold reeks of the ideologies colonizers brought into the lands they invaded to justify their conquest. It is the same ideology that says the gospel in its purest form is found in the Western church, an ideology that persists in mission organizations and drives their appeal to young Christians. In order to be a part of a mission movement that truly glorifies God and honors his creation, we must understand the long history of such practices and confront their unfortunate legacy. Chau's tragic story is the result of a theology that pities and belittles non-Western cultures to the point of their death. The idea that "unreached" people don't know what they want when they refuse a Western approach to sharing the gospel with them stems from the "primitive peoples" ideology that paints people of color as less-than or animal-like. Jesus didn't model a forceful gospel that we shove down someone else's throat; look back at chapter two and Philip's approach of the Ethiopian eunuch. The drive to make converts layered with assumptions in this outdated process led us away from the call to make disciples and to a direct violation of human rights.

The notion that tribal people do not know God because of their isolated lifestyle is the first conclusion Western Christians gravitate to. This assumption negates God's general revelation of himself and his common grace to all people around the world: "For his invisible attributes, that is, his eternal power and divine nature, have been clearly seen since the creation of the world, being understood through what he has made. As a result, people are without excuse" (Romans 1:20). It also places the "missionary" as the authority for confirming salvation. Labeling people groups as "unreached" because they haven't been colonized and Westernized is a dangerous fruit of the doctrine of discovery, which has been and continues to be the foundation of the movement to contact uncontacted tribes.

Surely we can't believe that God is so small that he awaits Western theology and white saviorism to reach his people around the world. Our understanding of how God works is limited by our humanity, our culture, and the stories we've been told, especially in the mission movement—a narrative the West has controlled for centuries. We have lost the capacity to imagine that God's general revelation could lead people to Christ. In fact, the main way Christianity has been spreading in Muslim countries is through visions and dreams, with Jesus Christ himself revealing himself to them. Yet the Western approach to sharing the gospel starts from imposing its norms on others rather than asking what's normal to them.

Scripture shows that the disciples proclaimed the gospel through humility, persecution, and years of service using culturally subversive methods. Nowhere in Scripture do we find Jesus using force to get people to follow him; quite the contrary—he lets people choose between him and their comfortable lives, and if they choose the latter, he leaves them alone: "If anyone does not welcome you or listen to your words, shake the dust off your feet when you leave that house or town" (Matthew 10:14). We have been given freedom to love, honor, and respect people and their boundaries as we share the gospel. Western evangelization efforts tend to focus on celebrating salvation professions rather than life transformation through discipleship. In gospel work the means don't justify the ends. We worship and follow a holy and just God who would choose the persecution of the laborers over the suffering of the community being evangelized. Yet we continue to expand our evangelical agenda at the cost of cultures and people groups losing their identity while being forced to embrace a Western culture and educational system that benefits capitalism.

WESTERN IMPERIALISM

The disciples lived for the expansion of a kingdom that required only the spilling of one innocent man's blood for the salvation of all. This kingdom requires no more blood to be spilled to make it whole and asks no man to kill, steal, or destroy in God's name. Of course, we are called to die in defense of our faith, but we are not called to kill for its sake. The word *missionary* is viewed negatively by young Christians because it represents people who push their beliefs and culture on others. In order to allow the next generation of Christian leaders to wear the name "missionary" as a badge of honor rather than a shameful rag, we must reconcile the past of Western imperialism with the present and create a platform for truth and justice to live together.

In 1879 for the first time in America's history Native Americans were recognized as "persons" under federal law. This took place nearly four hundred years after Christopher Columbus claimed to have discovered the Americas and that the land was inhabited by "savages." The dehumanization of the natives reinforced the idea that they were not worthy of possessing a land filled with such potential. It excused the colonization of the land by white settlers and the countless massacres that took place in order to take it over in the name of God—the doctrine of discovery in action.

Mark Charles defines the doctrine of discovery as "a set of legal principles that governed the European colonizing powers, specifically the administration of indigenous lands to the present day. The principle emerged from fifteenth- and sixteenth-century decrees by the pope to enforce Western theology and white supremacy, justifying violence, genocide, and slavery in the name of Christian evangelization. The doctrine of discovery provided a theological foundation for the assertion of white supremacy."[2] Dehumanization comes before cruelty because it emboldens and excuses the savage act of the perpetrator. It was essential to characterize Native Americans as savages instead of as fellow humans wearing a different shade of skin and equally created for community before taking over their land. Dehumanization serves as a weapon to silence the still, small voice inside the perpetrator that identifies another human as an image bearer of God while excusing their suffering. It took more than two hundred years for their humanity to be acknowledged by law in their own land, after their extinction and generational trauma.

The same doctrine of discovery was used to colonize Africa. In fact, there is a saying: "When the missionaries came to Africa, they had the Bible and we had the land. They said, 'Let us pray.' We closed our eyes. When we opened them, we had the Bible and they had the land."[3] This, too, is part of the legacy of Western missions around the globe, one we must confront before we shift our focus to the next movement of mission. A reckoning must take place to root out the problem Western Christians are facing so that the unity of the global body of Christ doesn't become stunted.

This practice of going into communities and imposing one's culture, language, and religion without understanding the local context is still being carried out today. Although many organizations try to provide crosscultural training for those going, most of the materials designed to train missionaries are prepared by Westerners for Westerners. How do you learn a culture accurately secondhand? Shouldn't these trainings be given by the country's men and women? Biases and blind spots are bound to affect the way we view others, and when our perspective on mission is shaped only by Western culture and its lens, we can only do so much. As believers who seek to spread the gospel around the world and carry the mission, we must understand the doctrine of discovery and its implications for diversifying the mission movement. Viewing God, ourselves, and others through its lens dictates how we interact with other cultures. It is our responsibility to understand how this doctrine has historically excused the physical and spiritual abuse of Black and Brown people around the world while building capitalism for the West at their expense. If we don't do the hard work of uncovering where this doctrine lives in our churches, institutions, and interpersonal relationships, our presence in a land that is not ours in the name of doing "missions" is at the very least a threat to the livelihood of those we encounter.

The doctrine of discovery reinforces not only societal biases but also spiritual assumptions that view the spiritual practices of those it seeks to dominate and colonize as evil and inferior to its own version of Christianity. In the United States, "religion was the key to the founding of a number of the colonies. Many were founded on the principle of religious liberty. The New England colonies were founded to provide a place for the Puritans to practice their religious beliefs. The Puritans did not give freedom of religion to others, especially non-believers."[4] It is ironic that the spiritual liberty of one group of people came at the cost of the spiritual oppression of another. Our understanding of America being a Christian country stems from this idea that it was "founded" on Christian ideologies, when in fact the land was stolen from the people who were here first, and Christianity was used as a weapon against them. I think we can conclude that true Christianity that forsakes the world and pursuit of its possessions was not what we're discussing here. It makes one wonder, What kind of religion did the colonizers practice that allowed them to kill and destroy image bearers while they freely practiced their own religion and built an economic empire for their people? This doesn't sound like the gospel Jesus died on the cross for. It certainly isn't why the disciples were martyred—quite the opposite. We can see why there might be resistance to a faith that didn't come with the type of witness Jesus and his disciples displayed. To me, it looks and smells like the prosperity gospel that has taken over the global evangelical church.

True Christianity should honor and protect human lives, their possessions, and their cultures. It also should respect boundaries imposed by others; they are, in fact, experts concerning their own livelihood and culture. We must have the self-awareness to know we are servants of God who humbly do his work wherever we're welcomed to do so. We are not called to be invaders of national security or oppressors of people groups. That is not the gospel, nor is it the mission to make disciples around the world. Many Christians of color are leaving the church in America because as they dig in to their history, they're finding unsettling truths about how the faith they love so much was introduced to their ancestors. They are experiencing a sense of betrayal that history was buried in the past without reconciliation. When they are challenged with worldly ideologies that say Christianity is a "white man's religion," they falter because the evidence shows that it is indeed a white man's religion. At least here in America it has been established as such. There is no path built to reconcile the past with the present and show that Native Americans did worship God before the white man came or that Africans are among the oldest Christian communities in the world. Not talking about this issue or shouting "critical race theory" every time the topic is brought up will only make a way for the enemy to further divide the church. Christ indeed died for all and he is not owned by any one culture, but Western Christianity fails at proving that fact to people of color who are questioning their faith.

The doctrine of discovery is still impacting us. It informs how institutions we are proud to associate with were birthed and are run to this day. For example, consider the debate over whether Christians should distance themselves from the term *evangelical*. Brown and Black Christians in America are choosing to do so because the word has cultural and political implications and serves as a stumbling block to their witness of the gospel in their communities. Movements such as the Jude 3 Project should be credited for creating spaces for Christians who want to distance themselves from the stained past of evangelicalism. They provide a space to hear the gospel apart from its association with oppression and colonialism. Ideas such as the deconstruction of faith and orthodoxy with justice emphasize the need to reexamine our Christianity and uproot the evil of the doctrine of discovery that we once embraced in the name of Jesus. It's only fitting for Christians from all backgrounds to understand the implications of how the gospel has been presented by Westerners around the globe. It has made Christianity appear to be a religion that can be practiced only when other cultures adopt and make white culture their own. We cannot move forward with an inclusive movement of mission for the next generation of Christian leaders without identifying and removing all remnants of the doctrine of discovery.

SINGLE STORY

We know for the most part how imperialism has impacted Black and Brown people, but let's explore its effects on white people. White Christians with an imperialistic gospel have been robbed of their ability to see other human beings who are made in the image of God as equal. White saviorism, an outgrowth of imperialism and the doctrine of discovery, is one of the greatest threats to authentic community in the mission movement. Romans 12:3 tells us, "For by the grace given to me, I tell everyone among you not to think of himself more highly than he should think. Instead, think sensibly, as God has distributed a measure of faith to each one." My heart grieves for those who are unable to see a person of color as someone from whom they have much to receive because I know what they miss out on.

The ability to see God from another cultural perspective not only emboldens our faith but leaves us in awe of the majesty of the king we worship. When we go to heaven we expect to be in constant awe and wonder of the king because our eyes will finally be able to see him in his whole splendor and glory. While on earth though, he has given us the diversity of cultures, languages, and even food to give us a glimpse of his splendor and glory. Diversity is the lifeline to a vibrant and unapologetic faith that is empowered by the Holy Spirit and is ever evolving. We can have a faith that is as exciting and awe and wonder filled as God intends for us, if we would allow him to reveal himself through others he has made in his image and be open to new aspects of his glory that our own limited culture is unable to reflect.

When churches use pity as the driver of mission in white people, they stir God's people away from his desire to sanctify them in the process. They automatically become the helper and miss out on the opportunity to be helped. To me, pity is worse than hate. Hate might cause you to distance yourself, but pity gives you good-intentioned proximity that might cause you to smother the object of your pity to death. Isn't that the cyclical nature of white saviorism wrapped in the gauze of good works in the current missions movement? It is suffocating, not empowering, and it absolutely is *not* loving.

In her TED Talk "The Danger of a Single Story," the famous Nigerian author Chimamanda Ngozi Adichie calls this a "patronizing well-meaning pity."[5] It's a dangerous position for white Christians to be in when thinking they are extending compassion or love to another human being while they're in fact patronizing them. If we truly examined where this pity came from, I'm willing to bet it would be the subconscious sense of superiority that was taught to white Christians from childhood. A sense of "I have it better than everyone" robs one of the ability to be an equal member of the global body of Christ. It creates a false identity that one has to have the loudest voice and always be in charge, proceeding from an assumption that only I have something to give.

In the same TED Talk, Chimamanda highlights the need for more stories to be told from Africans' perspectives, underscoring the diversity and beauty of growing up in Africa. She says, "If I didn't grow up in Africa, I too would have thought Africa was a place of beautiful landscape, beautiful animals and an incomprehensible people fighting senselessly and dying of AIDS, unable to speak for themselves and waiting to be saved by a kind white foreigner. This single story comes from Western literature." I couldn't agree more. I think about the mission books I have read over the years. In stories of the missionary "hero" and primitive Africans, the focus is more on the goer and less on the one who sends, as well as on those who receive and welcome the stranger into their midst. To comprehend what it takes for the receiver to welcome a stranger into their culture you can look at the immigration reform conversation in America.

The word *Africa* can have several meanings to the hearer, depending on race, ethnicity, age, and gender. Thanks to Bono, the ONE Campaign, and the celebrity fad of adopting African children in the 1990s and 2000s, there are generational differences in how Africa is understood. These well-intentioned efforts did some good work by addressing the immediate need of hunger, but for the most part they attracted the wrong attention. They reinforced a stereotype that everyone from Africa has AIDS and all the children are orphans. The Christmas song that wonders, "Do they know it's Christmastime at all?" is an example of these stereotypes.

Depending on when you were born you might have a certain assumption regarding Africans as well. Many baby boomers were raised with the single story of Africans as savages who needed the gospel by any means necessary, even slavery and colonization, because the end justifies the means. Gen-Xers mostly know Africa from the single story of the poor, helpless, and least of the least. They read stories about how they could change lives by going there. They were told that going to Africa was the most selfless act they could undertake, and maybe if they dug a well or two, they could save some souls. Millennials have read and cried over books like *Kisses from Katie*, and they know Africa from the single story of orphans waiting for thousands of Katies to come and rescue them. They have "felt called" to open orphanages and clinics even though they know nothing about raising kids and have no medical degrees. They have believed "one kiss could change African kids' lives." Many millennials have gone on short-term trips just so they could hold babies, kiss their faces, and make them smile, as if a smile were something that could come only from an encounter with a white savior.

Generation Z gives me hope, as I've seen them be shaped by the idea of Africa as Wakanda, home of the superhero Black Panther. They are confused about what their role in going would be, since Wakanda doesn't take kindly to white saviors, and Gen Z is quite aware of that. They're thinking, "Um, maybe they should come here and teach us a thing or two"—at least I'd like to think that's where Gen Z is headed. I am encouraged by Gen Z's resistance to the status quo, resistance to submit to colonial views, and zeal to experience God through his justice and mercy. I'm thankful they keep saying no to what doesn't honor God and are holding off on signing up for mission trips that feel void of the true mission of Jesus Christ.

Nigerian priest and missiologist Francis Anekwe Oborji asks, "Is Africa good only for promoting outsiders to hero status? The impasse here rests on the fact that many people easily associate material deprivation, technological simplicity and skin color with spiritual needs. . . . Since Africa has the highest number of the world's poorest countries, it must logically follow that it is the place where the unreached are found. When missiologists are convinced of this, an inevitable link between mission and charity develops. Mission and charitable work become synonymous."[6] In fact, mission should be about discipleship. These biased frames we look through close off the door for us to learn about cultures from the people themselves. The ability to learn about the God they worship from their own mouths and experience how he has revealed himself to them is the very spiritual enrichment the enemy is trying to stifle in white Christians.

It seems to me that Western theology has intertwined financial poverty with spiritual poverty and is producing disciples of the religion of capitalism. It's dangerous to send an army of missionaries into the Global South where the Spirit of the Lord is moving vibrantly without providing proper theological training that is able to see Jesus apart from physical comfort. Being a human by itself gives us an inherent wealth. Interacting with souls Jesus died on the cross to redeem should make us hesitate to call them the poorest of the poor. All humans on earth are worthy of respect because God made them in his image, Jesus died for them on the cross, and the Holy Spirit desires to reside in their hearts. There is no poverty in that. No matter what their physical conditions are, they are worthy of honor. As Paul considered himself the worst of sinners, we must look at ourselves as the least of the least and leave God's people to him.

THE GAP IN CROSSCULTURAL RELATIONSHIPS

This single story has been told and retold for centuries. It has taught not only white Christians but all Christians to idolize white missionaries. It does so at the cost of pitying Africans and indigenous groups around the world that are assumed to be unreached. The question "Does anything good come out of Africa?" seeps through the many interactions I've had with white Christians in my years of vocational ministry in the United States. It's hard to form a relationship with someone when you see them through the single story you've been told about them. What good is a relationship if one party has already made up their mind about how to treat the other? If they think they know what the other needs without asking them?

White children are implicitly and explicitly taught that they're better than people of color. A simple statement such as, "Do you know there are children in Africa dying of hunger?" to a child who refuses to finish their dinner implies that the child is somehow better than those in Africa. As youth, they are also placed in controlled environments created by faith institutions in the form of short-term missions. They are continuously exposed to Black and Brown people who are in far less ideal conditions than them. When they return home their interaction with people of color is nonexistent, affirming their suspicion that they are in fact better. Their parents have no friends of color, their role models don't reflect the diversity of the world, and the only time they interact with anyone who looks different from them is through charity. They learn by association that all Black and Brown people are poor and less than them. This reinforces the idea that the reason they are financially well-off and living in better conditions is that they're a better race, loved, chosen, and blessed by God. We can only expect that their interaction with people of color outside of that controlled setting will play out as being either a white savior or an authority figure needed for the betterment of these communities. The power dynamic indigenous missionaries struggle with in their work is a result of this cycle, which the West thinks is a mission movement. They are expected to lead "mutually," when everything around the mission organization is shaped and dictated by a structure that doesn't favor their leadership.

In contrast, most people of color in America go through life acutely aware of the injustices around them and experiencing microaggressions. When I first noticed I was being seen as another, I blamed myself. I thought it was because I wasn't picking up the cultural cues fast enough. Although I spoke fluent English and made every effort to fit in, I was still an outsider and a subject of interrogation. There were several instances when people couldn't control the urge to pet my hair. This created great confusion for my newly forming understanding of social norms in crosscultural relationships. It was not only invasive but also raised questions about their level of self-awareness: "Who do they think they are to touch my hair?" I'm not saying this to be snarky. Think about it: American culture glorifies personal space and privacy. It would be against the social norm to hug a child one just met without any relational context for the gesture. So when they lifted their hands to my head simply because they had a sudden urge, it showed me they had no regard for my dignity, no fear of repercussion, no interest in building a relationship. When it came to my personal space, they had no problem breaking the norm typically extended to others like them. Their interest was in satisfying their curiosity—touching the hair and knowing how it felt was their main objective. There was no regard for the person whose scalp was growing the hair, who wore it as their crown, and who didn't let anyone but loved ones touch it—to give it love, to nourish it with oil, and to braid it with tenderness.

This foreign touch felt rough, evoking an unpleasant emotion from day to day. I didn't know who would suddenly approach me with this "uncontrollable urge," as they described it, or when it would happen. I felt unsafe in spaces that didn't include people who looked like me. They behaved similarly to how my toddler does when he finds something that fascinates him, grabs it, and examines it with all his senses. If he doesn't like it he throws it away, but if he's pleased with it he plays with it. That's how I felt when I was touched without my permission and probed by questions that were intrusive and one-sided, without expectation of reciprocity. I felt like a token or, if I was "lucky," a trophy to be shown to others—just like when my son proudly brings me something he deems worthy, saying, "Look what I found!"

Hair represents a great deal in many cultures and is almost universally considered a vulnerable and tender area of the body. It holds a sense of honor, history, and intimacy, and it is only for loved ones to touch. One cannot be naive enough to touch it without permission and expect to be embraced.

Funny that I never had that same urge about their hair; never did I rush to touch hair that appeared flat and straight at all times. As foreign as it was and as much curiosity as it sparked in me, I wouldn't dare invade someone's personal space and touch one of the most intimate parts of their body without permission. One of my best friends who is white loves to have people run their fingers through her hair, so I've done that for her while comforting her after a tough day. It was a special honor to experience the texture of her hair on her request. I knew I was trusted with it because I had earned that place in her life. Never have I felt such a unique sensation. I experienced how straight hair runs differently through my fingers. It felt foreign, but it was just hair, and my touch had a purpose: to comfort.

We are not made to objectify one another; we are made for holy community, to equally reflect God's beauty to one another. The vibrancy of the church of Christ depends on her diversity; there must be room for every tribe and tongue to fully be at home in her. These simple encounters can draw us closer to one another or push us further from each other.

The journey toward true mutuality is hard work for all of us, but it may be especially difficult for a white person who holds a missiology shaped by the doctrine of discovery. People and places are not to be "reached" to conform their understanding of God and his Word to our liking. They must be reached so they can be taught his Word in order to continue to worship the God they know in their own context. We must believe God's Word that says he reveals himself to everyone and that all people are without excuse. Our work in discipling the nations is about finding out how God has already revealed himself in their culture so we can give them access to his written Word if they don't have it. When we start seeing God's people as already loved, chosen, and contacted by the Creator, we can unburden ourselves from the heavy weight of reaching the "unreached." Our role can shift from invading their culture and safety to learning about how they see God and expanding our own worship of him through their eyes. In our effort to evangelize and convert, we miss the opportunity to change ourselves and be captivated by God's glorious work in different cultures.

Relationships are the key to community, and if the mission given by our Lord is to go to the nations and make disciples, we need to do it through deep human relationships that are long-suffering and honoring to God and one another. Think about it—that's exactly the reason Jesus left his glory to become one of us: to see us as we truly are in all our complexities and to understand the depth of our humanity. He chose to experience life through our perspective and take on himself God's judgment that was to come on us. The outcome of his life on earth gave him an unbiased, well-informed, and real relationship with humankind that moved him to deadly obedience on the cross. In Philippians we see the degree to which Christ humbled himself. How much must he desire to be close to us in that he left his glory to pursue a relationship like that?

> Adopt the same attitude as that of Christ Jesus,
> who, existing in the form of God,
> did not consider equality with God
> as something to be exploited.
> Instead he emptied himself
> by assuming the form of a servant,
> taking on the likeness of humanity. (Philippians 2:5-7)

The beauty of it all is that we, too, are called to that type of relationship, marked by sacrifice and long-suffering, but we can't get there if we objectify each other. We are not made to idolize or enslave one another; we are made for community with each other so we can worship the king together.

FOUR

CONTEXTUALIZING THEOLOGY

Mission is the mother of theology.

MARTIN KAHLER

I INTENTIONALLY PICKED AN EASY MAJOR as an undergrad because I was dealing with severe homesickness and culture shock, and I reasoned with my nineteen-year-old self that I didn't need another headache. I didn't visit my family for three-and-a-half years, and I was emotionally depleted being in a new country on my own. I had been through enough to know I couldn't handle a rigorous degree that would require a lot of emotional labor. Communication came easy to me. I loved to write, read, and speak on topics I was passionate about. So, I thought to myself, why not foster the gift God had already given me? It was one of the most critical decisions I had to make by myself as an adult, and it is one that has brought me much joy.

During those formative years I paid attention to everything about the new culture I was immersed in. I somehow figured out that free food and football played a huge role in forming community in my Christian college. I also noticed the complexity of American Christianity, with its multiple denominations and rivaling theories of theological correctness. I remember attending a debate on the topic of Arminianism versus Calvinism and thinking, *What in the world are these people doing?* The differences in how Christianity was practiced perplexed me, because I definitely came from a different scene.

In Ethiopia there are three major denominations of Christianity: Ethiopian Orthodox, Catholic, and Pentecostal/evangelical, which would be considered Protestant. That was it. Even though we had different practices within the Protestant circle, everyone who was part of it would say they were Pentecostal/evangelical or a born-again believer. No one denomination would debate theology within itself—that would be seen as a public declaration of the instability of its belief systems. We might have had an Orthodox priest debate with a Protestant pastor, but even then it would be private, not something on display as a form of entertainment or a type of bizarre intellectual sport. There was a sense of honor and awe for the name of God and how it was brought up. This flaunting of knowledge of him as a way to obtain victory over someone else was odd and seemed vain to my taste.

BEYOND INTELLECT

Ethiopian Protestants distinguish themselves as born-again to signal that we believe in the gospel of Jesus Christ for our salvation. Filled with the Holy Spirit, we believe in the active works of the gifts of the Spirit as they were found in the early church. That's one of the major distinctions between

Protestants and older traditions of Christianity in Ethiopia. Believers are known for living vibrant, Spirit-filled, and transformed lives. I wasn't able to find that version of Christianity in my new home, America. I didn't know how to tell who believed what because the differences in theology were tedious, seeming to have more to do with intellectual preferences than the power of God at work in each person. It seemed like the focus was not on how much fruit believers bore but rather whether they could argue their way through Scripture.

I had professors from different backgrounds too— Pentecostal, Southern Baptist, Baptist, Presbyterian, and Quaker—and to say I was confused about these many variations was an understatement. I couldn't conceive of the idea that these traditions would come together and teach in the same college while they debated their ideologies on stage. It was quite the experience, something that further taught me that Western theology is concerned more with contextualizing theology for itself than for other cultures. I saw the process of contextualizing theology to the point of presenting it as a sport for intellectual stimulation. Although it was bizarre to me, I saw that it worked for the audience. Quite honestly, I grew to appreciate the different ways God revealed himself in each tradition and had opportunities to experience him in different ways. This broadened my view of God and grew my understanding of his greatness.

Even though at times I questioned why these people were so impassioned about something that was nonessential to salvation, I learned that in their context it was everything. While studying rhetoric with one of my favorite professors, Dr. Grave, who came from the Quaker tradition, I discovered the idea of contextualizing theology to culture, and I fell in love. My interaction with this professor was one of the main tools God used to draw me into ministry in a Western context. It gave me nuance to see myself and others through a more measured lens. He kept my interest piqued by his impeccable lectures and his unique ability to call out the good in each student. He was the first American professor who saw potential in my writing and speaking abilities, and he helped me develop and own my voice. When giving me feedback on papers, he encouraged me to tell more stories that affirmed the value of my experience, because he believed it added to the perspective I was sharing.

He'd say, "Make sure you don't leave your country, your people, your culture, or your experience out of the story. Your background should inform how you look at the world." He taught me that looking like everyone else was not the goal and pointed out how my unique voice was one that needed to be heard as I wrestled with the message of assimilation coming at me from everyone else. The Lord preserved me in a foreign place while sanctifying me through people like him.

I felt valued and appreciated, so in response I delved more deeply into the theory of rhetoric, which led me to love and understand theology better. This new love for rhetoric pushed me to press into my ability to think deeply and make educated arguments as I presented my points. I loved it. I could naturally argue a point till I was out of breath, and now I had tools to support my natural gifts. The freedom to think how God made me to think and not let myself be pushed to assimilate in my thoughts allowed me to become an independent thinker. I felt emboldened to question things that didn't line up with

Scripture's interpretation in my cultural context or apply to the theology and missiology of my land. My whole reason for coming to America and going to a Christian college was so that I could go back home better equipped to minister among my people. So I had to make sure everything I was learning could be applicable where I was going.

Dr. Grave's classes were an escape from the reality I faced elsewhere. The politically charged evangelical space I didn't know how to navigate became more bearable. I started reading about the denominations I interfaced with through my professors and studied how their theology informed their approach to loving their neighbor and their ability to teach me without bias. Each of us has a culture, which means each of us comes with a worldview that informs our reality. The concept of rose-colored glasses helps us understand the sense of value placed on an individual's lived experiences. Coming from a collective culture, I never prioritized my individual wants and needs. I craved the opportunity to look into my experience and understand my worldview as informed by my Ethiopian upbringing, so as I took more theology courses, I worked hard to reflect on my culture. I started seeing things I hadn't noticed before, confronting ideas I may have held close to my heart before being removed from my normal habitat. In my culture I had to worry about what I said, what I wore, how I carried myself for fear of how it would reflect on my family. That's how my culture of power-fear and honor-shame has shaped me to view the world around me. Everything I did affected everyone around me, and my success or failure was everybody's business, so I struggled to please everyone.

Living in the West away from my community meant I was free from that communal responsibility, which felt like a burden for a teenager who just wanted to think about herself. I'll be honest: in the beginning, I let out a sigh of relief to experience America as an individualistic culture. The simple act of going to a restaurant to eat by myself would have incited many questions from bystanders back home, but not here—no one cared. It was freeing. I loved the idea that I could finally discover who I was and what I could be without worrying about the impact it would have on those around me. I thought I could explore the world, dream big dreams, and not care how everyone would react. I loved the simple freedom individualism offered me, not having to answer to an elder in my community about why I changed my major for the third time or why I didn't want to be a doctor, lawyer, or engineer. It was liberating!

But the honeymoon phase didn't last. I soon learned that the silence I was enjoying from others had another edge. When silence is used as a response to pain, it attacks with an excruciating sense of loneliness, and that was a new feeling for me. Especially once I started challenging the status quo in white evangelical spaces, silence became a frequent response, which I later learned was typically used as a weapon of oppression.

This silence expressed itself in many ways, but I remember the first public rebuke of silence I experienced when I brought up the topic of gifts of the Spirit in my New Testament class. We happened to have a temporary professor that week, and he rushed through Mark 16:17-18, where Jesus says to his disciples, "And these signs will accompany those who believe: In my name they will drive out demons; they will speak in new tongues; they will pick up snakes; if they should drink anything deadly, it will not harm them; they will lay hands on the sick, and they will get well."[1] This particular topic of signs and wonders is one I hadn't heard a sermon on since I had moved to the United States, so I really wanted to slow down and understand what my new community thought about it. I was especially interested because I had noticed that our worship experiences seemed restricted and prayer gatherings felt more "dull" than what I had been used to back home. Emboldened by my interaction with my rhetoric professor, I decided to engage this temp professor with questions I simply wanted answers to. After all, it was a learning environment created to shape young minds for the kingdom, right?

I raised my hand and asked if we could talk about those verses. I added that I never hear anyone preach on topics like these anymore and shared how we talked about them frequently as part of our discipleship back home. These passages were taught as part of bearing fruit as disciples of Jesus Christ, that the powerful lives we lived were accompanied by signs and wonders. There were no ifs, buts, or maybes. It was important for me to understand in detail if I was going to effectively study what it meant to be a disciple of Christ and apply it to my context.

I expected the professor to say, "Well done, Mekdes, for pointing out how our experiences inform our theology. Let's dig in." Instead the man looked at me with irritation and a sort of pity. My classmates seemed confused about the relevance of my question. The professor eventually responded, "Maybe we can discuss that another time." Then he added, "We don't believe that in our denomination."

It felt like I'd broken some type of social norm and that he disapproved of my question. I remember feeling shame, a sense that this topic was inappropriate in this circle. This created further questions and confusion in my mind: Who did he mean by "we"? Was he talking about the school? The country? All Christians? Who did he represent? My culture and context demanded an answer, because in Ethiopia we experience God's powerful and miraculous works daily, and many have given their lives to Christ because of the freedom they have found through his power. God uses dreams, visions, physical healing, and signs and wonders to appeal to his people so they can abandon all other "higher powers" and follow him. Even if the latter part of Mark 16 is contested by theologians because some manuscripts don't include these verses, there is evidence throughout Scripture that the gifts of the Spirit are vital to furthering the gospel: "This salvation had its beginning when it was spoken of by the Lord, and it was confirmed to us by those who heard him. At the same time, God also testified by signs and wonders, various miracles, and distributions of gifts from the Holy Spirit according to his will" (Hebrews 2:3-4).

In my community it's not sufficient or even appropriate to argue intellectually with people who have had pagan worship experiences. Believers must be equipped to show others how to follow a power that is greater than what they worship and help them abandon evil for good. In my crosscultural evangelism training I talk about the focus fear-based cultures have on the power of God and how the way we share the gospel needs to start with highlighting the power of the resurrected King. Our context needs a rescuer who is not only good but also more powerful than what we've experienced, and dogmatic theology doesn't fit in that context. Philip Jenkins's observation of paganism points to the problem:

> Pagan and primal religions teach the existence of spiritual menaces facing society, but they also provide means to combat those dangers. A crucial flaw of early white missionary activity in Africa and Asia was that it forbade these solutions, whether amulets, fetishes, spells, charms, or ceremonies, since all were conspicuous symbols of pagan practice. At the same time, though, missionaries rarely offered plausible spiritual resources to combat what were still universally seen as pressing menaces.[2]

As recorded by Tibebe Eshete, the Ethiopian evangelical movement grew exponentially after the Communist Party kicked out all Western missionaries and the Ethiopian evangelical church went underground. In fact, because there was no pressure to practice Western theology from missionaries who were religious authority figures, local leaders gained the freedom to contextualize Scripture, and during hard persecution came spiritual revival. In that context the church grew and Ethiopian evangelicalism moved away from Western theology. One of the main outcomes was the freedom to practice the gifts of the Spirit, which enabled leaders to exercise deliverance ministry to free those enslaved by evil spirit practices.[3] That freedom also made a way for theology to be taught in a way that our oral culture could grasp and pass along to others.

The movement went from written theology to oral through gospel songs, which mirrors the Ethiopian Orthodox Church's practice of *Kidase*, or liturgy. To this day the greatest theologians of our country are gospel singers. Our morning prayers start with gospel music; we use that as our devotional book per se and start reading Scripture based on the theme of the song. The Ethiopian evangelical church is big on intercessory prayer, and in her theology on suffering, there is a clear call to die to self and live for Christ that cannot be missed. This movement includes witch doctors who have given their lives to Christ and later became leaders of the church.

The stories I could tell are many, but my point is this: we cannot leave out the power of the Holy Spirit and achieve the same goal. The days of persecution and the existence of the underground church are not a distant memory for us. They were just a little over thirty years ago, which allows us great proximity to giants of the faith who kept the church alive while being imprisoned, some even giving their lives for her. That's why when I hear of "theological famine" in Africa, it breaks my heart for the Western church. It breaks my heart because I see the depth of self-idolizing theological practice in the Western church, which demands creating mini versions of herself. It also breaks my heart because it reveals to me a deep level of unpreparedness to learn from brothers and sisters around the globe. It tells me that her ears are deaf and her eyes blind to seeing Jesus powerfully depicted in other cultures. I know it grieves the Lord's heart to have a disjointed body, especially one that is concerned only about the practice of Western theology and not about the global work of God.

THE CENTRALITY OF SPIRITUALITY

The Western church is so busy characterizing Africa as a spiritually dark continent that she's blinded to the darkness in her own body. We need to pay attention to how African theology is demonized just as Africans are dehumanized. If you look at some mission organizations, their mission and vision statements proudly announce how they go to places that are spiritually dark. By definition, a spiritually dark place would be a place where the Spirit of God does not exist. And that is not possible because God is everywhere, and he has revealed himself in nature. Therefore, there should not be a spiritually dark region apart from God's reach. This idea further paints Africans as primitives and dangerous people who are helpless without the white man's touch of grace.

There is a dark spirit called Satan, and he resides and works in every part of culture and language. Those who are not of Christ will experience spiritual darkness in their hearts and lives, which means people in spiritual darkness are everywhere, including America. If we geographically designate Satan to one part of the world, we're not only theologically incorrect but also missionally ineffective. We are blind to the darkness we and our neighbors experience each and every day right around the corner. A simple look at the number of African believers and the exponential growth in churches on the continent tells me a different story. I see a spiritually vibrant and beautiful continent that is being called on to go and make disciples of all nations, especially the West as Christianity is declining.

In the past, the Western church might have been able to point her finger at Africa and claim that witchcraft and voodoo were found only there, but that's not the case any longer. Things like witchcraft, communication with spirits through mediums, and astrology are widely practiced in Western culture. It's easy, for example, to sign up for an

Ayahuasca retreat, where psychedelic drug use is central to help the "brain break free of the body" so the message of the world is loud and clear. They preach their own gospel:

> There are many ways to reach the truth of non-selfhood. Think of it as a mountain peak, with meditators and certain spiritual traditions ascending different sides. Psychedelic drugs offer a kind of shortcut; you get a glimpse of this higher truth without all those years of serious, disciplined practice.[4]

These experiences are promoted as the best way to work through childhood trauma, and young Europeans and Americans are embracing them. Yet the church of the West says nothing about this; there are no books, sermons, or trainings that are preparing believers on how to address these issues.

I am not a scientist and cannot speak about the scientific aspects of Ayahuasca, but I know that the moment we start having spiritual experiences without the Spirit of God at the center, we are opening dangerous doors to the enemy. "Do not turn to mediums or consult spiritists, or you will be defiled by them; I am the LORD your God" (Leviticus 19:31).

When I find myself in conversations with people who have been through these spiritual experiences, I lean heavily on the teaching of the Ethiopian church I grew up in. It allows me to share the gospel without reducing the power of God to just a head knowledge that doesn't address the root of the issue. God is a God of spiritual experiences and is more powerful than whatever these people experienced. He is mightier than a one-week psychedelic retreat. Unfortunately, the Western church doesn't do a good job of teaching how the

Spirit of God can move into our lives and how we can experience utter healing and freedom through him. We are taught to know the truth but not shown how to practice it. How can we disciple this generation without contextualizing the gospel for them and showing them the true spiritual practices that can address their deepest needs?

Many people in Western society claim they are spiritual but not religious. That in a nutshell means they're open to spiritual experiences whether from God's Spirit or other spirits. How do we preach the gospel to these individuals? The Romans Road won't cut it, nor will scholastic religion that does not address the desire for spiritual awakening they're seeking through their own spiritual practices. Western dogmatic Christianity fails to answer deep spiritual questions without the empowerment of the Holy Spirit. Our theology needs to provide God's church with tools to combat secular spirituality, and it cannot do that without embracing the Holy Spirit as he wholly is. That is what Jesus required of his disciples after he spent his most important three years of ministry with them. After he taught them everything they needed to know and gave them the command to go to the world to share the good news, he asked them to wait until they received the power of the Holy Spirit. An article written by Wesley Granberg-Michaelson states:

> Pentecostal and similar renewalist movements are growing at almost five times the rate of overall global Christianity. . . . For instance, it's estimated that throughout Asia there are 873,000 Chinese charismatic congregations. In Latin America, Pentecostals are growing at three times the rate of the Catholic Church.

And 44 percent of the world's Pentecostals are found in sub-Saharan Africa.[5]

This should be exciting to those of us who desire to reach North America with the gospel. The hope that comes from a gospel that is powerful because of the Holy Spirit is the only thing that translates head knowledge into a heart change. God is sending spirit-filled missionaries from the Global South to the West. Do our churches have space to receive them? As I write this, I imagine my colleagues either scared or getting ready to condemn my theology. Understandably, this is a territory most Western Christians don't have a context for. But for those of us who come from the Global South, having a personal spiritual experience at the time of our conversion or baptism is not unique. I personally wouldn't have been ready to give up the world and follow Christ at sixteen without seeing his miracles in my life and in the lives of those around me. He sought me out in ways that addressed my deepest spiritual needs, and that was an undeniably unique and spiritual reality that I want every believer to experience.

What I regret the most with my cultural immersion into white evangelicalism is that I felt the pressure to leave my dependence on the Holy Spirit and follow a new version of Christianity that idolized theology and doctrine. Assimilation translated into being in a community that denied my lived experience and, more important, denied the power of God. From my experience, Western theology attempts to mute the parts of Scripture it doesn't understand—or doesn't want to understand. By that I mean that if they challenge deeply rooted cultural norms, then some verses get swept under the rug rather than recognizing that God is ready to be mighty in the challenges we face. There is beauty in accepting that we follow a God who knows all and in getting comfortable with our limited knowledge: "For we know in part, and we prophesy in part" (1 Corinthians 13:9). We are to follow an all-powerful God and worship him even though we can never fully know or understand his ways. There is a sense of wonder and awe about his deity, something unexplainable, something that makes us long to say, "Maranatha—our Lord cometh." Our pride in being believers should come from following a king who is beyond our comprehension. Being his children means we have a shepherd who leads us as we trust and follow him into the unknown.

Don't misinterpret my push for the power of the Spirit to be sought in the Western church as my saying the West is devoid of the Holy Spirit. The Spirit of the Lord resides in each believer, but there is a difference in being filled with the power that allows us to do the work God has prepared for us to do. The Black church's powerful expression of faith and long-suffering is a beautiful example of God's power on display in the West. These spaces feel like home to me, though I find them few and far between.

Most of my interactions are with Christians, like my professor, who are quick to silence and not disturb the peace of the evangelical circles I've been in. A slap on the wrist, an indication that my theology and knowledge of God before entering their space were invalid and that I must be "rediscipled." Unless my theology was colonized, there was no room for me to serve among the majority. The fear of retaliation from people and institutions I considered my community kept me quiet from expressing my faith the way I wanted to.

That cannot be how the West continues to treat missionaries from the Global South. And that is why white churches especially fail to serve as an oasis for the marginalized, the oppressed, the immigrant, and others.

THE DANGER OF DOGMATIC THEOLOGY

One theological topic I must discuss is cessationism. This difficult Western theology is at odds with African and Eastern theology. Ethiopian theologian Abeneazer Urga argues:

The Holy Spirit as well as his gifts have become neglected areas both in academia as well as in the local churches throughout the West. Demonology—if it is spoken about at all—is relegated to discussions involving [unreached people groups] or places like Africa or Latin America, as if Satan and his compatriots do not exist in the West (or perhaps they are simply a superstition to be dealt with among unenlightened and unscientific cultures of the Majority World who have yet to be civilized). The Church in the West has too often succumbed to the lure of Enlightenment philosophy, thus positioning herself to engage in Enlightenment-influenced methodology and theology. The Enlightenment influence has far-reaching implications on the mission field. Missionaries . . . strive to make disciples among the nations. Those overly disciplined by Enlightenment thinking tend to some extent to become overly secular themselves, and then tend to produce disciples who are prone to syncretism.[6]

This is the danger of a dogmatic cessationist movement that puts God's power in a box and stresses that unless we see it, feel it, describe it, define it, and analyze it, we cannot ascribe to it. This belief system must be examined if the Western church is to rise up and reclaim her place as providing hope to the hopeless and offering healing from physical and spiritual illnesses. Western theology needs to reexamine its understanding of the Holy Spirit and his work, apart from the Enlightenment that has shaped secular culture. According to Timothy Tennent:

> Even though the deity of the Holy Spirit was resolved by 381, discussions about the exact nature and relations of the Trinity continued for almost a century. All of this had a profound cumulative effect on theological discourse in the Western tradition concerning the Holy Spirit. Because ecumenical discussions about the Holy Spirit were focused primarily on his deity and his relationship within the Trinity, there was a serious neglect of a full development of his work. . . . Several vital aspects of his person and work were neglected in post-Reformation Protestant theology in the West.[7]

This gap is one that can easily be filled by integrating the theological teachings of the global church of Christ. Latin American and African theologies have specifically grown in this area and have much to offer the West. Theology is not God's Word! Theology is our study of God's Word and how we look at God through our lived experiences. It's perfectly understandable why a theology that values knowledge would be the theology of those who've been shaped by the Enlightenment. The Western church has certainly offered many benefits to the global church, especially its emphasis on translating the Word of God into every language and promoting biblical literacy. But it shouldn't stop at that.

David Wells defines theology as "the sustained effort to know the character, will, and acts of the triune God as he has disclosed and interpreted these for his people in Scripture, to formulate these in a systematic way in order that we might know him, learn to think our thoughts after him, live our lives in his world on his terms, and by thought and action project his truth into our own time and culture."[8] One of the struggles for Western Christianity is that it is dominated by the theology of white men and the study of God from their perspective. Only that perspective is deemed worthy of being taught and is spread around the globe as "correct theology" without regard to the context and culture of the people it seeks to reach. Thus it colonizes the theology of the world and erects a modern-day tower of Babel, proclaiming Western theology as supreme and the standard to be built upon by all cultures.

I haven't seen efforts being made in the global mission movement to study theology from ancient churches in Africa. Even though Athanasius of Alexandria predates Thomas Aquinas by almost a thousand years, we hardly hear of his contribution to theology. Theologians and seminarians need to incorporate the works of ancient and contemporary global theologians to be relevant and successful teachers of the Word. One reason white pastors have only white flocks in their congregations is that their theology comes from one perspective: the Latin roots that produced Western philosophy. However, even Latin theology has its roots in African fathers such as Augustine, Cyprian, and Tertullian. But modern scholars de-Africanize these church fathers by claiming they were not Africans, thus perpetrating another form of colonization.[9]

Terms such as *theological famine* are used to describe the Global South's theology and presumed lack of it.[10] These terms not only perpetuate the "primitive African" narrative but also create a sense of intellectual superiority that says we don't have anything to learn from them. Kenyan theologian John S. Mbiti once asked Western theologians:

> We have eaten with you your theology. Are you prepared to eat with us our theology? The question is, do you know us theologically? Would you like to know us theologically? Can you know us theologically? And how can there be true theological reciprocity and mutuality, if only one side knows the other fairly well, while the other side either does not know or does not want to know the first side? You have become a major subconscious part of our theologizing, and we are privileged to be so involved in you through the fellowship we share in Christ. When will you make us part of your subconscious process of theologizing? How can the rich theological heritage of Europe and America become the heritage of the universal church on the basis of mutuality and reciprocity?[11]

Theology that is not of the West is deemed as less-than, and many mission organizations won't even consider forming partnerships with local pastors who don't ascribe to Western theology. They fear the unknown, and they fear what they can't control. As with the gifts of the Spirit, they will not let themselves consider the unknown because their

Enlightenment theology dictates that they rely on their intellectual strength. How can we learn from each other if one side always demands to be the teacher? How can we build trust and mutuality when one side insists on making the rules? The same questions are echoed by pastors of color all across America. Look at the efforts that are being made by organizations such as the Crete Collective to fill the gap in theologically one-sided church planting. What a loss for those who refuse to seek to understand them.

The church of Christ is to be made up of all tribes, tongues, and nations, but Western eschatology falls short of reflecting the bride's wholeness, therefore delaying her readiness for the coming of the Groom. The church of the West still needs to be beautified, purified, and infused with the aroma of the theology of the global church. Western evangelicals have stunted their own growth by refusing to be informed by "outsiders." Do you worship the same God we do?

DON'T QUENCH THE SPIRIT

We can never be the ones who introduce God to other people because God has already revealed himself to them. Our denial of the Holy Spirit's revelation of God through signs and wonders is one we must question. "When the Spirit of truth comes, he will guide you into all the truth. For he will not speak on his own, but he will speak whatever he hears. He will also declare to you what is to come" (John 16:13). Our theological positions must never be so entrenched that they attempt to dethrone God from his rightful position in our hearts and enthrone our own intellect as the compass for our spiritual life and direction. This approach to mission incapacitates leaders of communities that have experienced his gifts, preventing members of those communities from forming their own theology and pursuing wisdom. It leaves them unable to shape and lead their congregations in an orderly manner. As beautifully stated in 1 Corinthians 14, God indeed has given us everything we need for life and godliness. Let's not attempt to discredit God's work in others because we cannot understand it.

Something I have found interesting in conversations about gifts of the Spirit is that in some cessationist circles they don't deny that the gifts of the Spirit can be experienced on the mission field, but they deny that these gifts can be part of our day-to-day faith journey at home. I get confused every time I hear that. I understand the charismatic movement has hit a rough patch in the United States, with financial scams and moral scandals surrounding famous televangelists and the rest of the church's desire to distance itself from that. But it would be a hasty generalization to assume that errors committed by these leaders reflect a theological error globally. In addition, the West shouldn't dictate how the rest of the world sees, worships, and follows God. God should be the only one who dictates his will to his people and the shepherds to whom he entrusts them. Our collective calling to make disciples who follow Jesus doesn't include making denominational kingdoms around the globe that become a breeding ground for institutionalized theological oppression that bears no fruit. Regarding Western denominationalism on the mission field, David Bosch aptly states, "Each denomination tried to patent and export its own brand of the gospel. . . . For all practical purposes God's Kingdom was here identified with one's own denomination."[12] This is the reality of today's mission movement—one that looks and supports only those who would embrace its denomination as their own.

For example, the largest denomination in Ethiopia is not one funded by Western churches or partners, and it is not an ideal candidate for funding because its theological stance doesn't mince words about the undeniable power of the Holy Spirit. I've had American pastors who desire to do "missions" in Ethiopia ask me if I could find and connect them with a denomination that would theologically align with theirs without realizing how imperialistic and strategically unwise that is. It's an attempt to go where they can further *their* mission of oversight and control, not an attempt to join God in the work he's already doing. I don't think that's what Jesus had in mind when he entrusted his whole mission to his disciples before they were scattered around the world. Cultural and theological assimilation devalues the diversity of the global church and silences the voices of local leaders by assigning only one Western theological authority as superior. How can we expect local leaders to take ownership of an imported theology and strategy that works fine in the West but has no fertile context to grow and bear fruit outside of it?

The sermons I grew up hearing my pastors preach included countless testimonies of my people experiencing miracles that led them to Christ. I've heard how Jesus came to them in dreams or sent someone to their village to share the gospel with them. There have been countless stories of how all of a sudden they found themselves speaking a different language on their arrival to a small village to preach the gospel. Many of them celebrate God's healing them from terminal illnesses that have not returned for decades. These stories shaped my theology; they're why I chose to follow Jesus. And it would be a tragedy if I let go of the very truth that led me to my Savior because I traded in my journey with Christ for the teachings of the Enlightenment.

A SECULARIZED GOSPEL

For the Western goer who reads this and thinks it's futile to argue about the supernatural, I want to say, the mission movement cannot survive without the power of the Holy Spirit being acknowledged in our practices. "This is the word of the LORD to Zerubbabel: 'Not by strength or by might, but by my Spirit,' says the LORD of Armies" (Zechariah 4:6). When attempting to do ministry in areas where people have to pray for a miracle so they can receive their daily bread from God, we must become one of them and experience his provision with them. White saviorism has been actively exporting a secularized gospel that has introduced the global church to a prosperity gospel that says, "Just follow Jesus and he will give you bread through us." In fact, Ethiopian skeptics call evangelicalism the rice and corn religion because they see its introduction as manipulative. That is not the gospel, and practices of secularism must be condemned.

According to the Barna Group, "Across the age groups, worship through song and praying aloud are seen as the central practices. Elders consistently rank the importance of a range of weekly worship expressions more highly, except when it comes to the Pentecostal or charismatic act of 'glossolalia,' or what is more commonly referred to as praying in tongues or prayer language. Meanwhile, over one-third of millennials (36 percent) believes this is an important expression that should be a weekly part of their worship experience."[13] This report encourages my heart and reminds me that this movement is going to be intensified as Gen Z starts to grapple with their experiences of faith. The coming generation is one that seeks diversity, inclusion, and equity. This includes the diversity of how we practice Christianity in different cultures. When someone with New Age spiritual experiences approaches them, they must be prepared to give a reason for the hope that they have when asked (1 Peter 3:15). And how can they without the power of the Holy Spirit? Without engaging in this topic they will not be successful, and the church must be a place where they can be properly equipped and discipled.

I've had several friends in white evangelical spaces share with me their curiosity about gifts of the Spirit but say they were ashamed and maybe fearful to talk openly about it with their family or church community. The subject was seen as "emotional," a "spiritual relaxation," or something lacking in sound theology. When I initially found myself in these conversations, I didn't know how to engage with them. I come from a place that never associates shame with experiencing God the way the Bible says we should, through his Holy Spirit. I was taught to celebrate being in God's presence. Our churches intentionally designated weeks of fasting and prayer, asking the Lord to draw us close to him and do his miraculous work in the Spirit. We had revival prayer meetings for this reason. We laid hands on each other and prayed for one another according to Acts 8:14-17.

I know it can be hard for many in the Western church to picture these Spirit-filled scenarios without feeling they must be "disorderly," especially those who were taught that order in the church must supersede all else. But what seems disorganized in Western culture might be normal in others. In fact, sweet and special encounters with the Lord can be hampered if we fear the unknown and demonize other theological outlooks. I believe the lack of open dialogue around topics like these and the silencing of curiosity have harmed the vibrancy of the Western church and its reach on the mission field. Our mission trips need to incorporate opportunities for goers to sit under local pastors' teachings and learn their theology. The time for the West to be the only teacher is coming to a close. It's time to listen, learn, and grow.

The future should be full of "learning trips," where Western pastors and ministry leaders are taught how to pray, fast, and abandon self-reliance to complete trust in the Lord, submitting, for a change, to the teaching of those who used to be the receivers of their charity and theology. In this way mission will truly become the mother of theology, being with each other sharpening and informing our theology together. The global body can in fact function as intended, the hand doing the feeding, the mouth speaking, the ear listening, and so on.

A one-size-fits-all theology must be questioned, as it is less fitting for the work of God's kingdom around the whole world. There was intention behind God's design for diversity, just as there was intention behind God scattering those who tried to build the tower of Babel and dethrone God. It prevents us from idolizing ourselves, our perspectives, and our cultures. It stops us from creating a cultural superiority that threatens God's supremacy. Our diversity helps us be enthralled by his glorious power, might, and beauty as we seek to know him through his expression of himself in the diversity of global theology. As believers we must seek out diversity because it is the very antidote to self-worship.

FIVE

DECOLONIZING SHORT-TERM MISSION

To hell with good intentions. This is a theological statement.

IVAN ILLICH

IN THE SPRING OF 1968, when Roman Catholic priest and philosopher Ivan Illich was addressing a group of eager young student missionaries in Mexico, he laid bare some of the problematic motivations underlying their efforts:

> Hypocrisy is unconscious in most of you. . . . "Mission-vacations" among poor Mexicans were "the thing" to do for well-off U.S. students earlier in this decade. Sentimental concern for newly-discovered poverty south of the border combined with total blindness to much worse poverty at home justified such benevolent excursions. . . . Today, the existence of organizations like yours is offensive to Mexico. I wanted to make this statement in order to explain why I feel sick about it all and in order to make you aware that good intentions have not much

to do with what we are discussing here. To hell with good intentions. This is a theological statement. You will not help anybody by your good intentions.[1]

In this address Illich shared the same sentiments as Jesus does when he rebukes Martha and celebrates Mary's faithfulness in Luke 10:38-42. To force our "goodness" on people while they are telling us what they need is the ultimate act of self-service. Martha, full of good intentions, went to the Lord to accuse her sister of sitting and listening while she worked so hard to serve him. His answer to Martha gives us a glimpse of what he still desires for us to do. One thing is required: to sit and learn at his feet and abandon the distraction of service that has become synonymous with mission—especially short-term mission, which the West insists is needed to spread the gospel while many in the Global South have grown to resent it.

Short-term mission is an adaptation of slum tourism, which became popular in the nineteenth century. *National Geographic* writer Christine Bednarz reports:

> Slum tourism is not a new phenomenon, although much has changed since its beginning. "Slumming" was added to the *Oxford English Dictionary* in the 1860s, meaning "to go into, or frequent, slums for discreditable purposes; to saunter about, with a suspicion, perhaps, of immoral pursuits." In September 1884, the *New York Times* published an article about the latest trend in leisure activities that arrived from across the pond, "'Slumming' will become a form of fashionable dissipation this winter among our Belles, as our foreign cousins will always be ready to lead the way."[2]

This leads one to wonder how many other things the church has welcomed from secular traditions and celebrated as good without questioning their origins as well as harmful effects. The mission movement has dressed up harmful practices in Christianese and continues to entertain Christians who want to be distracted by the feeling of doing something good without having to sit at the feet of Jesus. I must be fair and acknowledge that significant efforts being made in some mission organizations to do away with short-term trips. Unfortunately, what they're being replaced with might be worse. Physical poverty experiences are now being offered through virtual tours. Yes! You can now walk the "slums" virtually and experience poverty from a distance. I am not sure what the purpose is other than a change in strategy to do the same thing as before without seeming quite so voyeuristic. In reality it is still poverty tourism that does not bring about a holy change in the tourist's heart, nor does it honor the living conditions of sacred human beings.

THE NEED TO SELF-ACTUALIZE

As part of a society and culture built on the idea of the pursuit of happiness, the Western church tends to value the haves more than the have-nots. Specifically, white evangelical Christians are among the wealthiest members of American society, thus the church's struggle to attend to the hierarchical needs of her generous patrons. To understand this concept, I find Maslow's hierarchy of needs helpful. If we look at it from bottom to top, this tool helps us see the display of an individualistic culture's pursuit of happiness, which can be a synonym for the American dream.

This psychological theory states that unless people's basic physiological, safety, and security needs are met, they have no to little desire for other needs higher up on the hierarchy, including love and belonging, self-esteem, and self-actualization.[3] It tells us that the poor will not be motivated to give until they achieve a capacity for giving by first fulfilling their needs.

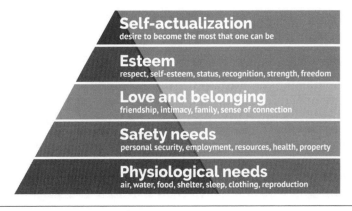

Figure 1. Maslow's hierarchy of needs

Maslow's hierarchy of needs has been used to shape broader culture and workplace strategies, to build motivation and establish a path for climbing the career ladder. If we look closely, this theory also underpins the way white evangelicalism has established its outreach efforts. Those at the bottom of the hierarchy of needs are taught that they have nothing to give to society and to their faith community. These communities are automatically categorized as receivers whether they are believers living on the margins here in the United States or around the globe. The people who are at the top of the hierarchy of needs can participate all along in outreach activities such as short-term mission. The ability to pay for one's trip (or at least have the network to raise money from), travel, and be able to take off one to three weeks from work are all essential to being a part of these trips. All these things require a certain level of financial and job security, something communities of color largely don't have. This secular theory assures those with means that they are called to serve because they can afford it, while it leaves behind those with less, reemphasizing an anti-gospel message that they must climb through the hierarchy of needs to be able to fulfill their Christian duties. This model is not all encompassing and therefore is not a biblical model.

Quite the contrary, in Mark 12:41-44 Jesus tells the story of the poor widow and her meaningful gift to God. What stands out to me is how he compares her gift with those of greater means; he deems hers more valuable because she gave out of what she didn't have, while the rich gave out of their surplus:

> Sitting across from the temple treasury, he watched how the crowd dropped money into the treasury. Many rich people were putting in large sums. Then a poor widow came and dropped in two tiny coins worth very little. Summoning his disciples, he said to them, "Truly I tell you, this poor widow has put more into the treasury than all the others. For they all gave out of their surplus, but she out of her poverty has put in everything she had—all she had to live on."

The text speaks for itself; the poor widow's gift was more pleasing to the Lord because it came from a place of complete faith that God would provide for her needs as she gave all she had to him. In doing so, she outgave every rich man in the temple.

We can all agree that the missions model mainly practiced by the West does not encompass all the economical statuses of God's people; therefore it is not a biblical model to follow. Until we are able to make room for all believers to be part of God's mission, we cannot begin to have the conversation about the next mission movement being from the Global South, where people have less disposable income to utilize toward travel and support of the West.

It is estimated that two million people go on short-term mission trips every year and spend about four billion dollars per year.[4] That figure is the same as Haiti's annual budget, for the whole country. If in fact the system was in place to serve the "poor" it would have worked, as there is no lack of finance or people willing to serve. But it is clear that it in fact serves the goer at the expense of the poor. Phrases such as "giving to the poor," "helping the least of these," and "giving a voice to the voiceless" often accompany pictures of Black and Brown kids being held by white teens. This asserts to one group of people that their self-actualization lies beyond the ocean where those struggling to find their daily bread live. They are sold a lie that God's desire for them is to go and be "the hands and face of Jesus," as if Jesus were not found among other economic circles and apart from their material possessions. Therefore we see a massive flow of mainly white people traveling across the world to make sure they fulfill the call to self-actualization, to *feel* used by God and needed by others.

A report by Baylor University states, "Students who participate in short-term mission trips tend to have lower levels of materialism, greater appreciation for other cultures and a better understanding of missions as a lifestyle. In general, the greater the amount of trip experience, the greater the impact."[5] This might be true, but it factors in only the impact on the goer of meeting the physical needs of the receiver. How about the spiritual and holistic well-being of the receiver? I do not agree with the idea that sending millions of people on mission trips somehow opens floodgates of generosity toward the poor. This presents God as having limited powers to provide for his people and being dependent on the ability of the rich to fill in a gap he cannot. If the rich have to witness financial poverty so they can be compelled to give, it's not the type of giving God requires of his children.

I do not believe that my people's salvation and liberation are tied to Western money that comes into our land at the cost of our dignity. I sure don't see that in the Bible. I see a gentle, humble, and relatable God who put on flesh and took on the most humiliating punishment possible for a sin he didn't commit so you and I could have direct access to him. It is a grievous sin to offend the work of the cross by minimizing it to a transaction: giving money to the poor in exchange for the betterment of our character.

Short-term mission trips are in fact about the goer, not the receiver. The instant gratification and long-term impact of achieving self-actualization help the goer sustain a self-image that keeps them going as they pursue their American dream. This dream says, "Work hard, play hard, give from your surplus, and make sure you get tax breaks for it." It doesn't demand that these goers fade in the background while Christ is exalted above all else. There is no sacrificial living required to go on a short-term mission trip. They don't focus on building relational equity, time spent with others that leads to adapting to a new home, or suffering through the discomfort of the unknown for the sake of the gospel. Short-term mission trips are the byproduct of a drive-through culture, a quick excursion to do what Western Christianity expects of us so we can check a box and go back to our lives of surplus.

EMOTIONAL MANIPULATION

Have you ever wondered why every short-term trip to another country starts out with a tour of the worst conditions possible? Dare I say it is still fashionable to take people to the "slums" so they can get the maximum emotional impact? Sadly, these emotional responses last only a few weeks, and they're based on a whole lot of assumptions and scant personal interaction. We miss out on God-given opportunities to building lasting relationships with others and settle for being agents for spreading the prosperity gospel. In any relationship we enter in life, first impressions are vital. They set the stage for how we feel about someone, which impacts our decisions regarding a future relationship with them. Short-term mission is a horrible tool to build relationships between two cultures because it exposes the worst living conditions of one group while it highlights the apex of white saviorism for the other. How then can these two groups operate as equals, mutual partners, and brothers and sisters in Christ?

Great disservice has been done for decades in the way these trips have been carried out. They are set up to make the most grievous first impression possible on the goer, characterizing the receiver as helpless and not equally made in God's image.

And the goers play God's role and try to frantically rescue, something they are in need of within themselves. These two worlds colliding do not lead to building true relationship, finding common ground, or mutually learning and growing. Their design is to emphasize extreme differences, with good intentions causing great harm. It's also deceitful because these trips condition them to only interact with one group of society from that country, leaving out its larger culture, history, politics, and everything else that makes up a society.

The result is what we see today: a never-ending cycle of white saviorism and economic disparity, as well as a large gap in mutuality of leadership. The system was not set up to create relationship but dependency on one another. You give me my self-actualization and I'll give you bread—that's what it was meant to do, and it has done its job effectively.

We cannot overlook the vital role videography and photography play in setting the stage for these interactions to happen exactly as they do. The goer has had an upper hand in studying the group it's going to go "serve" by the stories and videos presented from the perspective of a Western communicator. On the other hand, the receiver knows the goer either by the tales told in the community or by what Hollywood says about the West. These two groups have different preconceived notions about each other even before they meet.

In the documentary *Stop Filming Us*, brilliant videographers of Congo beautifully share their perspective of why they should be the ones telling the story of their own land. Confronting the idea of white saviorism, they express how tired they are of being represented by others who don't know who they are. They lament the death of stories in their community that have been forgotten and sanitized because they didn't meet the white man's standards. They express anger at the colonizer who comes in the name of healing Africa from the pain and destruction he himself created.[6] Image is a powerful tool for telling a story, and it's on the consumer to question if what they are being fed is truthful, ethical, and just to the subject of their interest. What we have right now is largely a manipulative and one-sided phenomenon that most indigenous leaders have no control over. Next time you have to sign a waiver or a permission slip saying yours or your children's pictures can be used as a promotional tool, think about whether the same privilege was afforded the Black and Brown faces you see on your church's wall. It's a simple protective measure afforded to children here in the States because we know how pictures can be used to harm them, but we seek out and exploit the most vulnerable children from other countries.

There is no lack of photographers and videographers who do an amazing job of telling their own people's story, but the world hasn't been exposed to their talents because of the way fully equipped camera crews from the West have invaded and dominated their market. This is something we cannot ignore. The rise in street kids in Africa is directly connected to "poverty tourism," a.k.a. short-term missions. These children leave their families in villages and travel to cities where they'll meet foreigners who give them money, a cookie, a hair tie, or take a picture of them. It doesn't matter what they get—they want proximity to the white savior and they look down on authority figures from their own communities. They remain poor, hoping to catch a white savior again the next day.

It is extraordinary to see how Maslow's hierarchy of needs reflects the Western church's view of salvation. The poor at the bottom of the pyramid clamor to receive their daily bread, and the rich at the top pursue self-actualization by capitalizing on the pain and suffering of others. There is no exchange of privilege for the sake of another. There is no walking in another's shoes or seeking to understand their life. There is simply exploiting another's reality to feel good about one's own.

TRANSACTIONAL VS. RELATIONAL

We can all agree that the Western church has some work to do to redeem her legacy of mission and transform it from transactional to relational. Transactional says, "I have something you want, but you can only have it if you give me what I want." Relational acknowledges, "I need you in my life, and I'm here when you need me." The former is a performance-based, loveless relationship that objectifies one group of people for the satisfaction of the other. The latter takes the performance pressure off and centers the humanity of both parties. Most of our problems would be solved if we could focus on building a relational legacy in our churches and with our mission partners. We would celebrate being our brother's keeper and truly live life as Christ did. A relational approach is the path to building multilayered coalitions of missional leaders throughout our churches, communities, and the global body. When we focus on relationships, everyone has something meaningful and attainable they can work toward. At this point, it's difficult to identify what's broken in the Western mission movement unless we're actively seeking it out and have an outsider's perspective to guide us. It is a disservice to the global body to continue to train Western church planters and missionaries with harmful strategies and worldly metrics to grow their reach. We reap what we sow, and if what we sow is a transactional seed, that's exactly what we'll harvest with what we might call our "mutual partners." These partners for the most part want nothing to do with Western theology that is so rigid that it contributes to the erasure of their cultures. But if we invite our partners to become true partners who help us contextualize theology so that their cultures are a big part of their faith, our involvement makes a way to birthing global church movements led by indigenous believers who can disciple their own people. These types of partnerships by those who truly view one another as brothers and sisters in Christ and who submit to one another's leadership bridge the gap that imperialism created in the global mission movement.

I, too, have been an accomplice in a movement that tries to enforce change in the name of making others' lives better. I have participated in mission trips I am not proud of. I did it assuming the method I was trained in was the only way for my people to see Christ. Living in the United States as part of a monolithic church culture taught me to assimilate by adopting its culture as my own and letting go of mine. As I grew in leadership within the church, the training I gained couldn't be applied to my cultural context, which made me ineffective in reaching my own people. With my colonized mind and overzealous heart for Jesus, I took a group for a short-term trip to my people in Ethiopia so they could "help" them. What I learned was that although we'd had many training sessions, my team was nowhere near ready to be in the presence of my people as spiritual leaders. They lacked a true understanding of the beauty of God displayed in Ethiopia and in the community we were visiting. The underlying assumption was that our lives were better than theirs and were something to aspire to. We were too focused on what we could do, what we could change, and how we could help them "escape" their realities. We missed out on what they were doing and saying to glorify God among themselves.

Short-term mission as we know it is largely a one-size-fits-all charity movement from the West to the rest of the world. For the most part, these trips are designed to place a heavy emphasis on countries and people groups that fit a particular church's vision and mission. There is little consideration of receiving a call or invitation from local pastors and indigenous missionaries to be part of what they're doing. Instead churches seek to go where they want to go and do what they want to do. Local leaders are given the role of distributor of whatever solution the West deems appropriate, and they play the role of intermediary instead of head or shepherd.

Jesus came incarnate with flesh and bones so he might understand us and be understood by us. But this Jesus is not represented in a transactional, short-term approach. His example of spending thirty years in a community before revealing himself as the Messiah and starting to minister is not replicated in these models. He was part of the people to the point that they rejected his message because they knew him as the carpenter they helped raise and not the Savior. But short-term mission has created a false God where people find their white savior for a week or so and then eagerly await his return the next year. This undercuts the reputation of true and faithful leaders in those communities who've been trying to earn their way into people's hearts.

I once went on a medical trip to Ethiopia as a translator for the team. The people of the village told me to get out of the way—they wanted to be cared for by the white people. They thought I was an impediment to getting direct access to the *ferenje*, as they called white people. They knew they'd get money or some type of physical need met. And they were right. They had figured out how the system worked: "I make the white people feel good and they give me food or money." When someone who looks like them gets in the middle, the machine stops working. In fact, I don't get gratification from holding their babies, because I hear what they're saying. It may be a mother who says, "Let them take the baby; maybe they'll give him a better life than I can, and he will one day come back and help his family." With this false sense of security coming from complete strangers, our people are conditioned to rely on these trips that undo all the work local Christian leaders have put in.

For my husband and me, choosing to support a mission organization has been a difficult journey because we know too well how culturally and spiritually unprepared people mischaracterize or demean our people. For the most part we have shifted our financial support from Western institutions that promised to end poverty to those that invested in indigenous leadership. We've also found many faithful indigenous pastors and organizations doing amazing work to redeem people's hearts for Christ through discipleship methods that were appropriate to their context. We have great relationships with local missionaries under Cru Ethiopia, SIL Ethiopia, and

EvaSUE (Evangelical Students and Graduates Union of Ethiopia). They are doing an excellent job of contextualizing the gospel and equipping capable leaders to serve their own communities. This is especially true of EvaSUE, an organization started and run by Ethiopians that has made a lasting impact on many students. The network continues to grow, extending to the diaspora community living around the world. These organizations are not asking locals to change their culture, language, or livelihood to follow Jesus. They are simply helping them understand how Jesus can make their broken world whole. They are slowly helping them grow into disciples who forsake all to follow Christ wholeheartedly.

This type of work takes years and years of dedication, a love and calling to become part of the culture, and a sincere desire to know and understand local history and language. We are blessed to have such faithful partners who continue to challenge our biases and humbly teach us. Not only that, but these brothers and sisters in Christ are the people we call when we have our own burdens to share. They are dedicated in praying for us and encouraging us in the Lord. These are the types of small but faithful ministries that are making an impact on the gospel movement around the world. If a short-term trip is needed to visit them, we don't take a large influx of strangers to go do something for them that they are perfectly capable of doing for themselves. We go to spend time with them, to pray with and for them as they do for us. This is what I mean by leaving a relational legacy, one that is fueled with friendship and trust because we have genuine and real relationships with God's people around the world.

TRAINING AND DEVELOPMENT

As discussed in previous chapters, the biggest problem in short-term mission trip planning is that the bar for recruitment and training of mission leaders is set lower than for discipleship leaders in our churches. The outreach pastor/department typically initiates a summer or spring break program and puts out a call for the congregation to participate. International, Western-led organizations are tasked with providing emotionally charged video presentations about the work they do. These images and stories evoke sadness and devastation in the assuming congregant, who now feels a deep sense of guilt for having it easy and "feels called" to go be part of this movement. It would be amiss not to point out that these videos almost always have children of color being cared for by white teens who are "bringing them joy." The need highlighted is typically a physical one because who in the West cannot meet a physical need, right? It's a very achievable goal to set for a middle-class white suburban Christian. The call to action is something to the effect of, "You can make a difference," or "This will change your life." After people sign up, they are immediately propelled into the training phase, skipping the typical ministry leadership development that would focus on character. The appeal is focused on the white savior and self-actualization.

The interview process is not as invasive as those that, for example, the volunteers in kids' ministry have to undergo. The mission trip leadership system does not have accountability built into it like what small group leaders need to abide by. The preliminaries are just a formality, a way of gathering information so we can follow up and get people through the system. When teams come together for training, they typically talk about what they'll be doing, how they'll pack for the trip, how fundraising is coming along, what accommodations will be like, and so on. It's like planning for summer camp, except they'll be going a little farther away and therefore need to prepare for their travels a bit more.

The most important step of making sure there is proper accountability is ignored in this preparation that is so centered on making sure the goer gets the most out of the experience. There is no representation from immigrant communities in the US that are specifically from the countries our churches travel to every year. In most cases these immigrant churches can be found within a ten-to-fifty-mile radius, yet an effort to build relationships with them is almost always nonexistent. Their input, wisdom, partnership, and blessing to go are all needed to make these trips somewhat helpful to the receivers, yet we continue to avoid building these bridges and impose our presence in a community we know nothing about.

When consulting on this issue, I give my clients five questions to answer before they decide to go on a mission trip. Why are you going? Are you connected to people in your community who are originally from the country or the community you seek to go serve? Have you sat under the teachings and leadership of pastors from that community? Is the organization you are going with led by local pastors and leaders? How long do you intend to stay? These questions help the goer decide if they have the right motive for going and if they have a holistic approach to mission that doesn't undercut local pastors' leadership.

Instead of teaching people simple greetings in a foreign language as a way of "equipping" them for their short-term mission, we can try another approach. Directing goers to worship in international churches in their cities planted by pastors from the very place the church "feels called" to go to would give them a more realistic expectation. There is a great advantage to having immigrant churches in our communities, as they can be the best training ground for the teams we send. Sitting under their teaching would add so much value to our congregations' ability to live a culturally enriched life at home before seeking it out on a mission trip. Time spent with believers from these churches would help set a realistic perspective and approach to serve their people well for the long haul. These churches are the underdogs in Western church leadership that are overlooked by large mission and church-planting movements. If looked at closely, they are the ones producing second-generation disciples who are uniquely positioned for the success of the multiethnic church. Fellowshipping with believers from all nations will allow us to break the barriers of racial, political, and ideological differences that our churches are struggling to overcome.

The task-oriented nature of short-term trips, which are void of intentionality in sharing the gospel and building relationships, deters even those "model minorities" who might have bought the idea and joined the movement, from going back. Almost every Black and Brown person I've spoken to about this topic has relayed how out of place they've felt on these trips. It's easy for them to clearly see the transactional nature of these trips that devalue the importance of taking time to build real relationships, which is central to communal cultures that they, too, are a part of. If we're honest with ourselves, we can easily see that sharing the gospel in a culture that is foreign, in a language we don't understand, and under a timeline that's limited requires somewhat of a supernatural ability in each goer. Can we confidently say those are the types of people that are among the millions our churches are sending every year?

In the New Testament where short-term missions are modeled by Paul, we see him staying at least three years in one place. During that time he plants churches, develops leaders, and hands it off to them to lead. When he goes back to visit, the intention is to encourage and build them up. There are no one-week tourist visits in the Bible that we can point to and say, "That's healthy." The missionary journeys we see in Scripture are almost always long-suffering, long-term, and selfless, whereas in our day, it's almost like there is an unspoken rule that says "satisfaction guaranteed."

A MUTUALLY BENEFICIAL FUTURE

A 2008 opinion piece in the *Wall Street Journal* reads,

> Today, many churches and mission programs are giving up any sort of economic justification for sending American teenagers to construct cinder-block buildings and treat people for head lice. Instead, they are billing the trips as "cultural exchange," "service learning" or "solidarity" ventures. This sort of rationale gets more at what the missionary philosopher Lesslie Newbigin re-ferred to as the Christian mission of "learning": "When he sends them out on their mission, Jesus tells the dis-ciples that there is much for them yet to learn, and he

promises that the Spirit who will convict the world will also lead them into the truth in all its fullness."[7]

I would argue that most churches have yet to adopt the philosophy of learning this piece talks about. There has been no drastic shift from "mission trip" to "learning trip." They're still heavily perpetuating the idea of, "Bring them food, and when they come for the food, give them the gospel." It is a transactional, "gotcha" method—one we don't see Jesus practicing in his ministry on earth. If in fact the emphasis is on learning, then it must start by learning from marginalized communities here at home before going around the world. Doing so will help us build a racially reconciled church that partners with Black and Brown church leaders and forges a healthy future for the global body. Somehow going elsewhere is still appealing because it gives goers the satisfaction of "spiritual growth" without having to confront their social responsibility where they are. It's an escape from their Christian civic duty that demands a transformation in them and their institutions. This is the very self-serving spiritual practice that what we must resist. By laying down power we will gain the ability to embrace mutuality. It is not easy, yet it's the necessary work we must do as Western Christians.

If we desire God's will to be done on earth as it is in heaven (Matthew 6:10), to see a glimpse of heaven while we live out our faith here on earth, we must consider a change in strategy. To worship God alongside his global body learning from one another without any expectations requires humility and equality. Just as each part of the body has its own function, I believe God is calling the Western church to be the ear, to take a listening and learning position instead of always trying to lead and teach. If it would, I believe the global body of Christ would experience the type of worship we see in Revelation 7, where we collectively cry out that salvation belongs to our Lord, but only when we submit to one another. Jesus never used his privilege; in fact he did not count equality with God as something to be grasped (Philippians 2:6). Yet we cling to a movement that glorifies the white savior—that teaches having money, power, and privilege is the only way to serve God. We fail to see the gift the poor in fact are to the body of Christ who give out of what they do not have but bring delight to the Lord. Submitting to the one who gave his life on a cross to redeem a people for himself from every tribe, tongue, and nation will need to include submitting to those who don't have the material possessions we may have.

The Western church has a long way to go to correct her missteps. Even though amended approaches such as learning trips are being suggested as alternatives to short-term missions, I believe there needs to be an even deeper shift. In my coaching program for Christian leaders, I share methods to decentralize missions. One of the ways is the incorporation of an annual vision trip at the end of the course that challenges Western missiology. Once leaders have spent a few months reframing their missiology, unlearning harmful practices, and exploring new ones, the program is designed to take them on a trip to give them an inside look into my homeland from my perspective. I call it "Ethiopia through my eyes."

I believe in this approach strongly because of how important first impressions are in forming mutually beneficial relationships. I want to have a say in how my people are being approached and create a platform for the locals to be their own storytellers. Minimizing assumptions, biases, or savioriorism by muting the microphone that centered only Western voices is essential. The goal for this platform is to give the upper hand to local leaders so they, for a change, can be the ones who choose their future partnerships. It aims to create a way for them to observe the character and witness of those who wish to work with them and decide if they're a good fit for their local projects. Whether it is sharing the gospel in their context or sharing solutions to social issues that will better the lives of their people, they are the experts. It's a selective and intentional process that is done by invitation only for those from the West because I'm a believer that not everyone should go. Maybe some are called to stay, and our sending process needs to help them figure out exactly where God desires them to be effective witnesses for the gospel.

If we are serious about correcting the past's transactional legacy and breaking the power dynamic that exists in the Western mission movement, we must be serious about decentralizing the movement. We must make a way for the power of the Holy Spirit to move mightily in the lives of his disciples that we're entrusted with shepherding, and we must follow where he leads. When individual believers are empowered by the Holy Spirit and supported by their spiritual leaders, they will certainly follow his poignant call to carry the gospel to the ends of the earth. No matter the cost, faithful followers of Christ will respond to what the Lord asks them to do. The beauty in that is there will be no need for spiritual and emotional manipulation that leaves them in bondage to self-actualization.

If the future of mission is to be defined by a solution-based, mutually gospel-centered approach, we must seek to understand the history, beauty, and traditions of the countries and people we desire to build relationship with. It's better for a Western Christian to first go as a real tourist and experience the finer things in a community through locals' perspectives before they go as a savior with nothing other than Westernization to offer. That way Westerners can have a different lens with which to view the people, their heritage, their leadership, and their pride as a nation. Going as a tourist not only offers a Westerner an ethically uncompromised trip to explore and learn about the country but also gives an opportunity to financially support the local economy in a way the economy is designed to operate. Learning the history from local professional tour guides and getting a version of history that hasn't been whitewashed or sanitized will equip one to become a self-aware and more sensible missionary.

As a way of ensuring good practices in short-term missions, I recommend these steps:

1. Visit the country of interest purely as a tourist. Engage the culture through the eyes of the locals; learn about their heritage and what defines them as a people.

2. Connect with believers in the community, visit local churches, and worship and fellowship with locals, making the goal the building of a relationship.

3. Collect data on what type of connection they have had with the Western church in the past. Ask what would most benefit the local pastors and leaders and ask them to provide potential solutions.

4. Present your case on how you would benefit from their engagement with your church and organization and make

sure it's more than mere cultural experience. Give them opportunities to teach, lead, and disciple your people.

5. Take only groups of people with the skills that fulfill needs presented by local leaders. Do everything you can to find local people with the desired skill set first and fill the gap afterward.

6. Leave your camera at home, even if it means leaving your phone at home. You can have the host take pictures, resulting in images that reflect their perspective. Better yet, hire professional photographers from the community and participate in supporting small businesses.

7. Limit or extend your stay based on the need and plan on going on a regular basis to support and encourage the work being done.

Unlearning takes time, and for the Western believer whose Christian service has revolved around mission trips, it is natural to overcorrect by completely stopping. Don't do this. I challenge you to read books written by local historians, economists, politicians, and faith leaders in a community you care for and assess what your specific contribution could be. If holding a baby and taking a picture is your only contribution, please volunteer at your local hospital or foster a child in your community. Don't spend thousands of dollars that could be used to feed and clothe foster children at home or support a full-time missionary abroad.

Removing some of the impediments to building trust on these trips by unlearning ingrained ideas allows both goer and host to experience the same thing. They get an opportunity to see God in a different cultural context and worship with a different part of the global body of Christ, which is priceless. This no-strings-attached approach allows us to see each other as people rather than as projects, and we can build community much more quickly this way. What's more, we can become an encouragement to the local body of Christ rather than a frustration.

Every good relationship starts from a place of mutual interest, mutual give-and-take, mutual understanding of the other's perspective, and mutual room to share grievances and reconcile. If one person or group has the power to alter the life of the other, that is not a mutual relationship, no matter how good the intentions are. Although God gave Adam dominion over every living thing, he did not give him dominion over humanity. Subtle remnants of the doctrine of discovery still exist in our partnerships that demand dominion, and they must be eradicated. Jesus prayed that that we may all be one in him as the Father and he are one with each other (John 17: 21). We are not called to have a parent-child or employer-employee relationship with the body of Christ. We are to function as one whole body of Christ, as colaborers and coheirs of God's kingdom. We need to make room for everyone to sit at the table, even those we deem less honorable. And if our partnerships don't reflect that, we need to take strong measures to insure they do so.

A diverse and beautiful picture of the body of Christ should inspire, encourage, and challenge us to strive to honor the parts we consider less honorable. There is in fact a greater value to be gained from what they can give the world, especially for the Western church.

SIX

THE SACRED COW: MONEY

For there was not a needy person among them because all those
who owned lands or houses sold them, brought the proceeds
of what was sold, and laid them at the apostles' feet.
This was then distributed to each person as needed.

ACTS 4:34-35

THE FIRST MEMORY I have of coming to America is the loneliness I felt after being picked up from the airport by a family member. I was driven to their beautiful home in the suburbs of Dallas, Texas. The loneliness didn't initially come from being homesick, since I had just landed and was excited about exploring all the amazing things awaiting me in America. It came from feeling like I was on another planet as we drove for almost an hour on highways and entered suburban neighborhoods where there was no foot traffic. It was an experience of isolation that seeped into my heart and left me wondering, *Where are all the people?* It was mind-boggling to see no sign of life. It was otherworldly and felt unnatural. Driving into a beautiful neighborhood with homes built out of bricks and rocks, I had mixed feelings. I didn't know at the time what it was—no doubt I was mesmerized by the beauty and cleanliness—but I also felt deeply confused at how artificial it seemed. It felt as if I were trapped in the Stepford Wives universe and couldn't get out.

Now that I have lived in the United States for over eighteen years, I have identified that strange artificial feeling I experienced when I came here. I now know that there was no sign of life because the needy were intentionally and strategically cast outside of these big and beautiful communities. The foot traffic I crave so much I can find in "inner cities" where community organically happens and people practice horizontal generosity.

> Beginning in the early 1930s, a ranking system designed to represent neighborhoods in northern and southern states was implemented as a means to ensure segregation of blacks and whites. The system included four strata from highest to lowest; A: green; B: blue; C: yellow; D: red. Neighborhoods that were integrated, containing Jews or foreigners, were given ratings of B or C. And those with any black presence at all, regardless of class, were rated D: Red. Hence, the term redlining. The consequences of such rating ranged from outright denial of mortgages to denial of home insurance to prospective residents of "Red" neighborhoods, thereby preventing black families the right to private housing, barring them from the very thing that provides security and wealth and confining them to neighborhoods designated by local and federal government.[1]

As I grew more aware of the social structure of America, I learned that my feeling of isolation had not only a name—redlining—but also a color—Black. It also had a long and devastating history of one group oppressing another and intentionally causing their poverty. In economics the term is *capitalism* and economically growing countries understand it as an unjust practice of power that needs the poor to remain poor so the rich can get richer. This capitalism is also very much in opposition to how the early church practiced generosity in Acts 4.

Let me say this before I go any further: it is possible to criticize capitalism without being a socialist. My intention is not to offer a new political framework but a biblical one. As believers we have a duty to take everything to the cross and examine how it passes the test of righteousness. When it doesn't pass the test, we need to file it under unjust causes that we either distance ourselves from or work toward rectifying. In communities like the one I grew up in, where capitalism hasn't shaped the social infrastructure, we are enriched by the experiences of people who are different from us. Living with one another lets us have neighbors who resemble what Scripture points to when it says, "Love your neighbor as yourself" (Matthew 22:39). A neighbor who is from a different tribe, has a different religion, or has a different financial status is still part of the community. When we honor those the world discards and deems shameful, it shows that we are followers of the one true God who has placed the *imago Dei* in all humanity.

REDLINING

After college I joined an internship program with McLean Bible Church in Northern Virginia, where I spent a year with like-minded young leaders. We were intentionally discipled and rigorously trained to become the future leaders of the church. This program included a mission trip where the group would go and spend about ten days in a needy community. Again, because we didn't have the needy among us, we had to create an outreach program to address the natural need of humans to share with those who do not have. In the past these teams had gone to Uganda, Haiti, or the Dominican Republic, but my batch was assigned a local trip to southeastern Washington, DC.

I was relieved, as I did not want to go on an international mission trip because of reasons I shared in the last chapter, but also because I was still on a work visa and nervous about leaving the country and the possibility of being denied entry upon my return. I thanked the Lord for his divine intervention and prepared myself for this one-week experience just a few minutes away. Our church had started an amazing afterschool care program that was run by local leaders, and it was serving the community in beautiful ways. Our job was to support the staff, clean and organize the space, and provide the kids with a fun-filled week. I was excited and honestly felt encouraged to be able to go to a place I'd never been. I naively assumed this area would be no different from the places I had lived in the last six or seven years in the States.

We took the metro orange line from Vienna, Virginia, switched to the green line at L'Enfant Plaza, and got off at the Anacostia River stop. Before we exited the metro station, our leader informed us to stay close to each other and walk fast till we got to the afterschool program home. As soon as we got outside I felt like I was in another country. I immediately noticed that the clean crisp look I'd become used to did not apply in this context. The gas stations were smaller and people could be seen huddled around the entrances, talking or just hanging out. What struck me most were the bars on the windows of the buildings. I remember feeling like I was inside a prison compound like the ones I'd seen in movies. I caught myself off guard when I blurted out, "Are we still in America?" I think my team was shocked by my question too, and without any answer everyone kept walking.

Call me privileged or sheltered, but that was the first time I had seen the missing piece in my experience of living in the States. It finally made sense: this was where the other side of capitalism lived. The promise of America was afforded to me, an immigrant, while it was kept from those who had built the country with their hands, lives, blood, and sweat. This was where America's famous proclamation to care for the tired, poor, and suffocated was secretly discarded. No longer did Emma Lazarus's poem about the Statue of Liberty apply:

> Give me your tired, your poor,
> Your huddled masses yearning to breathe free,
> The wretched refuse of your teeming shore.
> Send these, the homeless, tempest-tost to me,
> I lift my lamp beside the golden door![2]

The poem sounded like a taunting dream from where I stood. I couldn't believe my eyes. A country the world saw as generous, giving, and kind had a secret of its own. It actually had a habit of stomping on those who dared to rise and claim equality as theirs to possess. To this day I have that image embedded in my mind. Ten to fifteen minutes away the most powerful people on the planet gathered in the US capital to solve the world's problems, while these men and women struggled with generational oppression. My heart cried out to the Lord: *please make it make sense!*

That week I spent in DC I wondered not only whether I was in America but also why in the world Americans went to my country and the rest of Africa. I thought Americans came in masses to Africa because they had completely met the needs of those among them. It made sense to me when I thought about it that way, because that's what we're supposed to do as Christians, right? We take care of our neighbors before we go to other parts of the world. This new experience completely disrupted my view of mission work and helped me connect the dots between foreign aid work and missions. It also made me question the motives and strategies of institutions I had blindly trusted. The façade white saviorism put on as it walked my land was finally exposed. It treated my people as the problem, painting us as the poorest of the poor, the weakest of the weak, when in fact it was covering up a mess that needed to be cleaned up at home. Now I know why. Because those in the Western church haven't learned to love their neighbors as themselves, they fail to see my people as their neighbors and equals.

White Christians specifically must open their eyes to the reality that they have the comfort of the suburbs because of the existence of redlined districts in their cities. This classism built on income inequalities must end for these believers to truly practice brotherly love for all people. An honest look at history will show us how the rise of Black wealth was intentionally destroyed so that others could stay at the top.

> The [Tulsa] massacre, which began on May 31, 1921 and left hundreds of Black residents dead and 1,000 houses destroyed, often overshadows the history of the venerable Black enclave itself. Greenwood District, with a population of 10,000 at the time, had thrived as the epicenter of African American business and culture, particularly on bustling Greenwood Avenue, commonly known as Black Wall Street.[3]

The wealth concentration of America didn't stay with white people by accident, it was intentional. The "ghetto" doesn't exist by accident but by design; white flight doesn't happen by accident either. When Black and Brown people start moving into white neighborhoods, they're either met with hostility from banks with higher interest rates or homes start going on the market causing white flight.

The answer is not as simple as suburban Christians moving into lower-income neighborhoods. In fact, this can devastate these communities, who are forced to flee their homes as their neighborhoods become gentrified. The true work must be allowing them to flourish in their own communities by lifting systemically oppressive practices such as redlining. It is also questioning discriminatory loan practices and white flight that prevent Black and Brown people from moving into white suburbs. The existing separation prevents us from experiencing what Scripture points to in Hebrews 13:2: "Don't neglect to show hospitality, for by doing this some have welcomed angels as guests without knowing it." We shoot ourselves in the foot when we create distance between us and people from all tribes, tongues, and nations. We limit the church's ability to expand beyond one culture and miss out on seeing God through each other's eyes.

MY KIND

Being brought up in an economically growing country meant I was always around the needy. I regularly ran into people who asked for their daily bread when I was walking to school or driving to go meet a friend for coffee. In Ethiopia we call those individuals *yene bete,* a term that translates to "my kind" or "those like me." In fact, my parents scolded my siblings and me if we ever used the term *beggar* to describe someone in need. This term *yene bete* is used to acknowledge the *imago Dei* in others and remind ourselves that we are no different from those who temporarily lack material goods. This interaction didn't only happen on the streets; but also in my neighborhood because I lived close to those who did not look, dress, or eat like me as well.

Although, I grew up in an upper-class family and lived in a home with a compound surrounding the land we owned, not all my immediate neighbors lived as such. For example, we had an elder widow neighbor who built a shelter between two compounds right up our street. The two homeowners allowed her to stay there and looked out for her. She was part of many weddings, funerals, and births in our community, and all the kids including myself felt like one of her grandkids. My up-bringing ingrained in me that my role as someone who came from a family of means was to meet the needs I saw all around me without losing sight of their neighborly value. Some of my mom's best friends were women to whom she provided monthly financial assistance. She managed to be both a friend and a generous giver. There was no power dynamic at play, and this played a significant role in how I saw Christ. I learned that he was an equalizer. To me being poor is not a reflection of someone's eternal destiny or the condition of their soul; it's simply a lack of earthly possessions and a temporary state people can get out of at any given time. In fact, in my culture we talk about poverty mainly from a spiritual perspective. Parents pray over their children blessings such as, "May the Lord keep you from an impoverished heart" to signify their desire for our communal culture and legacy to live on in their family tree. The prayer was also directed against a life that lacks community, living in isolation and only with those who reflect our values, which presents the dangerous territory of self-worship.

The church's role is also clear when it comes to meeting the daily needs of those in want. Historically the doorsteps of the Ethiopian Orthodox Church have been a place where the hungry could receive a meal. In fact, when families are mourning the death of a relative, they go to the church to feed the needy at the doors as a way of honoring their loved one's memory. I actually had the opportunity to participate in this experience on my last trip to Ethiopia. We visited my paternal grandfather's grave and said our prayers. Both sets of my grandparents were Orthodox believers; therefore we honor their memory by following the traditions they honored, one of them being remembering the poor whenever they went to church.

Jesus in fact addresses the poor and their belonging in Matthew 26:11, after the disciples have accused Mary of Bethany of "wasting" perfume on him when it could have been sold and the proceeds used to feed many people. Jesus responds by saying, "You always have the poor with you, but you do not always have me." It's evident that he was not after the eradication of material poverty; he was after the eradication of spiritual poverty. He was basically telling the disciples that feeding the poor without showing the proper love and devotion to him was meaningless. Jesus advocated for and demonstrated a generous and practical approach to meeting physical needs while he celebrated an extravagant display of affection and sacrifice toward him. He chose Mary's act of worship, which seemed so wasteful to others. But he understood it as a sacrifice of her most expensive possession, elevating him higher than any other idols she may have had before he came into her life. And that was more pressing to him than feeding the poor at the moment. His prioritization of our devotion to him before meeting the physical needs of those with poverty shows us that our gifts and offerings without true worship mean nothing to a king who has everything.

Today we have secularized churches that glorify generosity to the poor but do not disciple their people to offer their love and affection to the Lord by sacrificing their idols. They do not condemn the time, devotion, and worship given to worldly pursuits that bring no joy or honor to the Lord. Quite the opposite, they reward the pursuit of idols by granting people seats at tables they have no business being at, as long as they bring the financial means to support the ministry.

Financial generosity cannot replace the relationship Christ desires from us, one that is filled with affection and that causes us to sacrifice our most expensive possession and pour it out at his feet. Instead the Western church has become an accomplice in assisting millions of undiscipled Christians who pour out their gifts at the poor instead of the King. It assists the enemy in distracting them from worshiping God and allowing them to preserve their unjust practices, making a way for them to keep the idols they don't want to sacrifice.

VERTICAL VERSUS HORIZONTAL GENEROSITY

In addition to informally giving to the poor, Ethiopia has another traditional practice called *iqub*, in which people pool their funds regularly to rotate loans among themselves. Participation is completely voluntary, and *iqub* benefits its members by offering large loans without requiring collateral or physical assets. This tradition is practiced in other African countries as well. In Nigeria they call it *sousou*; in Somalia it is *hagbad* or *ayuuto*; in Jamaica it is known as a "partner." In Guyana it is a "box hand," in Haiti *min*, and in South African *stokvel*. Kidist Yasin of the Lilly Family School of Philanthropy discusses *idir*, a parallel practice to *iqub*:

> Unlike the dominance of the wealthy donors in giving overall donations in developed countries, Ethiopian philanthropy, like in many other African countries, is mainly characterized by horizontal giving. In Ethiopia, *idir* is a grassroots social network and a leading traditional institution through which people help each other. It is a widespread institutional form in the country in which members make a regular monetary contribution

and provide labor service at the time of need. Although the main purpose of *idir* is often limited to covering funeral expenses and comforting families at the time of a loss of loved ones, some *idirs* are flexible and help people while they are alive.[4]

Iqub and *idir* are two financial pillars of Ethiopian community that we still rely on even in the diaspora community. They serve in place of things like life insurance for families that cannot afford to pay premiums. Plus, the money is guaranteed to come back to the giver, unlike insurance, which is an "in case of emergency" safety net that most people hardly ever use.

Communal giving allows communities to take care of each other instead of seeing people drown in loans that are increased by interest. It gives everyone a chance to benefit not only from financial assistance but from a community who comes alongside in a spirit of camaraderie. Usually in *iqub* a name is drawn from a hat so that the recipient of the gift is random, but when there is a dire need in the group, it's common to shift from the drawing of names to prioritizing the family in need. That month the family in need benefits from the lump sum of money but is still able to put a portion toward the next month's drawing. This allows the family to participate in the giving as much as the receiving. This protects the dignity of the receiver, a philosophy that is embedded in African culture. Not only are financial needs attended to but also emotional and communal needs. It is about caring for the whole person, as money alone cannot buy happiness.

This approach also reflects the beautiful horizontal philanthropy the early church practiced as seen in Acts 2:44-45: "Now all the believers were together and held all things in common. They sold their possessions and property and distributed the proceeds to all, as any had need." What differentiates selfish giving from selfless is what the giver receives. Vertical philanthropy offers the giver legacy, elitism, even huge tax credits, while horizontal philanthropy offers deep satisfaction, a sense of belonging, and a collective responsibility to help those around us. As believers we desire a relational legacy over a transactional one and must work our way back to God's heart for giving.

Western philanthropy, which is mostly vertical, can be dangerous when it moves into communities without contextualization. It tends to champion top-down charity, which exalts white saviorism. This approach makes its focus a sense of satisfaction for the giver, which is a selfish motivation of self-actualization. It comes at the cost of the receiver, which is a sure way to destroy the relational aspect of money and its ability to foster connection with others. "This kind of reciprocity is characteristic not only of American missionary work, but also of American philanthropy more generally. Donors require recipients. The more appreciative and grateful that recipients are, the more successful donors feel. And the more visible this success, the more the donor's own status is advanced in the eyes of both peers and beneficiaries."[5] It is in fact very American to pursue personal happiness even while performing selfless acts such as giving to the poor. One must ask a question, then: how can I give in a way that is selfless? And when I do want something in return, can I be honest about it with myself and others?

Conversations about distrust between donors and recipients on the mission field are constant and daunting to local leaders who want to have a voice. The problem is that Western philanthropy thrives on exporting generosity without having to wrestle with what that generosity looks like for the receiver on the ground. It also lacks practical proximity with those it gives to, even here in the United States. There is a clear social and economic segregation in America that's evident to see. As an outsider-insider I can clearly see it, while the lines might be blurry for those who haven't experienced generosity in another context. In the horizontal model explained earlier, philanthropy cannot exist without relationships and accountability. It demands an equal seat at the table and affirms that the one giving today will be an equal recipient tomorrow. There is a built-in balance to power dynamics in this approach, which welcomes more people to be participants.

Approaches such as microfinancing are helpful tools that have proven to work well to address the financial challenges in developing countries, while inviting Westerners to participate without creating chaos. Microfinancing is a system of loaning money to people with low incomes so they can start small businesses and get out of debt. It is a great way to support a growing economy; as a result, its methods have been championed by leaders in those economies. Nobel Peace Prize laureate Muhammad Yunus, who founded the first microcredit organization, says microfinancing organizations—or "social businesses"—have three characteristics: they aim to address a social problem, they are financially self-sufficient, and they do not pay dividends to owners:

> Yunus sees social business as an alternative and potentially more useful way for philanthropists to place their

money: Rather than making a one-time donation, they can invest in viable businesses generating recurring benefits. Potential profits are reinvested in the business endeavor itself rather than paid out to its owners, allowing to expand the produced positive social impact.[6]

This is a great way for Western donors to participate in helpful giving without hurting the very people they mean to help.

On the other hand, vertical philanthropy by design is void of relationship, so it's forced to make assumptions about those it gives to. It analyzes and diagnoses problems and offers solutions to problems it doesn't have experience with personally. A simple example is the recently instituted US holiday of Juneteenth. Even though it seems like a generous-minded act, the Black community's response has been less than enthusiastic, which has puzzled many whites. In fact, activists have condemned the gesture as putting the cart before the horse. The gift misses the point, as the main request from the Black community has been that reparations be made for the generations of physical and economic disparity imposed by slavery. Taking a day off from work one day a year creates no progressive economic change. Most Black people say they want reparations, not a pretentious holiday to rid white people of their guilt. This tension and lack of accountability are avoidable in horizontal philanthropy, which helps communities move toward mutuality.

If you give to a mission organization, you can spend as much or as little money as you want and find instant gratification. It's guaranteed that you'll be able to check a box and feel you've done your part without understanding the ramifications of your action. The general assumption is that if people are poor they need money; therefore you cannot go wrong with giving. In most cases this kind of giving is done in response to a story that's been told about someone you've never met, and you have no way of understanding the nuances of their livelihood. Giving financially is easy and it's satisfying. However, top-down philanthropy is an open door for foreign ideologies, political control, influence, and power to flood into economically vulnerable countries. Most importantly, it's a way for the enemy to preach prosperity gospel, linking the way out of poverty and finding prosperity to white saviorism, which overshadows the gospel.

As a foreigner doing crosscultural ministry in a Western context, I find it easy to see the gaps in the way American churches address poverty. Studying the history of philanthropy led me to its interconnectedness with missions. In fact, Protestant missionaries are considered pioneers of American philanthropy:

> The efforts of missionary leaders . . . emphasize the thematic connections between philanthropy at home and abroad. Charitable missions to the world extended abroad the various domestic discourses of promoting social betterment. . . . International activities such as the SVM [Student Volunteer Movement] were initially rooted in this Christian evangelism, but many gradually developed a more secular, professional-scientific cast, from which emerged models for the greater governmental involvement in philanthropy that would occur after World War II.[7]

"Social betterment" is the focus that has taken over the modern mission movement. We have replaced our call to make disciples of all nations with saving the world from hunger and disease, a secularized approach to mission.

To be clear, if we can do the latter while fully engaged in our first calling, which is to further God's mission to redeem a people for himself, it would be a beautiful thing. But to pursue the latter at the cost of the first would be a loss not only for us but for those we claim to have a heart for: "For what will it benefit someone if he gains the whole world yet loses his life? Or what will anyone give in exchange for his life?" (Matthew 16:26). When the Bible talks about loving our neighbors as ourselves, I highly doubt Jesus is referring to the way our suburban life is constructed here in the States. If you've visited any ancient city you will see that the poor and rich live among each other, making everyone your neighbor. The verse cannot be applied in its full context in our Western social, economic, and racial bubbles because we have built structures that shield us from experiencing true neighborly love. The type of philanthropy God has called us to involves confronting the evils of capitalism, racism, and classism and realizing we miss out by ignoring the injustice experienced by those considered needy in our own communities.

DECOLONIZING GENEROSITY

Although Western philanthropy is widely understood as a top-down model, it would be a disservice to the conversation not to examine how Americans of African descent have contributed to it very differently. In the book *Giving Back: A Tribute to Generations of African American Philanthropists*, Valaida Fullwood tells the varying perspectives of Black philanthropists. Her collection of work defines a philanthropist as "one who seeks to understand the human condition and responds to needs with financial and human resources," as "someone who recognizes the 'linked destiny' of all people of the earth and works beyond her or his self-interest to improve the quality of life for others. Everyone has the opportunity to be a philanthropist by deciding to live their life in a way that reflects empathy for others" and as "someone who cares and shows it."[8] These and many other definitions in her book put the focus on the humanity and relational aspect of philanthropy and not the transactional. As Scripture says, where our money is there our heart is also. Therefore when we invest in people our heart beats for them, while when we invest in our self-interest our heart looks out for what we get out of it. I believe that's the difference between vertical and horizontal philanthropy and why we have to decolonize our giving so we can invest in the humanity of others.

A good friend of mine who was starting to unlearn the Western concept of generosity shared with me that while she was walking into her bank to get some cash one day, she overheard a woman explaining that she wasn't able to meet her monthly rent and asking the bank for an extension on her credit line. The bank wasn't cooperative, and my friend felt the Holy Spirit telling her to pay the woman's rent that month.

What she said next got to me: "I found myself thinking I'd been taught to make sure everything was tax-deductible when I gave, and I was taught to make sure it was going to the intended place. This was a complete stranger who I knew nothing about." That thought interrupted the Holy Spirit's prompting.

My friend unfortunately decided to stick with what she knew rather than take a leap of faith and obey the still, small voice in that moment. When she told me that story, she was very disappointed in herself. I was not. I was happy she was at a point in her life where she at least recognized the harmful impact of institutionalized generosity and how it had prevented her from listening to the Holy Spirit. The only thing standing between her and her ability to show hospitality toward a stranger was her belief that her generosity had to be accounted for and traced for tax purposes. Even though she missed that opportunity, I'm sure the Lord will give her plenty of others, and I'm excited to see her unlearn a capitalistic model of generosity to truly do what the Word of God says.

We must wrestle with the fact that institutionalized generosity in majority white spaces may have moved God's church away from practicing biblical generosity. The idea that only the haves can give to the have-nots reinforces elitism and classism. It neglects the truth of God's Word that ascribes value to every image bearer, and it gives the rich dominion over the poor. It distorts God's command to every human being to rule the earth and subdue it no matter what their income level is. Instead, the rich hold their giving over the poor and insist that they do what they need them to do. The need to build bridges with Black and Brown churches is not merely to benefit them but also to benefit the white church that has become anemic for lack of reciprocity of the wealth the Black church could offer her.

Jesus was intentional in preserving the dignity of the receiver when he commanded his disciples to give. In Matthew 6:3 he said, "When you give to the poor, don't let your left hand know what your right hand is doing." This command is a rebuke of our highly controlled giving that guarantees a grand gesture of gratitude by the receiver, giving that not only gives but takes back in ways such as a building named after the giver or a huge tax break for further motivation to give. I strongly believe this approach is a hindrance to experiencing true biblical giving that produces reciprocity between giver and receiver and allows for true community and mutuality to flourish, and that is exactly what keeps Western culture from becoming communal. In collective cultures that elevate community over the individual, these types of organic and spontaneous giving are practiced widely. Although these gifts are not controlled and recorded, it doesn't mean that they don't happen. For example, the amount of money immigrants send back to their families and communities on a regular basis is not counted as a valid practice of generosity by Western standards. The Associated Press reports, "Money sent home by Mexican migrants rose 11.4% in 2020 to a new high despite the coronavirus pandemic. . . . Migrants sent $40.6 billion to Mexico in cash transmissions, known as remittances, including $4 billion in March alone, a record for a single month."[9]

If our churches were integrated and immigrant churches were legitimately recognized as an equal part of the American church, we would be in a better position to embrace mutuality and work with those on the receiving end. Those like the Mexican immigrants who are already financially invested in the betterment of their communities don't require a special missions appeal. The people who are already financially invested are in a unique position to be trusted and embraced when they preach the gospel. The American evangelical church is barely a witness to marginalized communities in her own Jerusalem. There are burned bridges with pastors and leaders of communities of color that need to be repaired before she seeks to go farther to Judea, Samaria, and the ends of the earth. The need to reconcile and be a witness is far greater at home than the need to evangelize abroad for the American church.

If in fact the American church continues to specialize in creating an experiential oasis for white Christians while helping them avoid racial reconciliation with their brothers and sisters, God's call to go to the nations will stay stale within her walls. The church must push out of her four walls and build bridges that seek true community with people of color. White, Black, and Brown Christians living in A: green; B: blue; C: yellow; D: red neighborhoods coming together to worship the Lord and meet each other's needs should be reflected in the churches' expressions of worship. Spiritual leaders have a responsibility to redirect their congregations' desire to isolate from communities of color at home while they "deeply feel connected" to a person of color in a different country. It is in fact a necessary spiritual correction that might require rebuke and accountability as Christians learn to reconnect with their neighbors and do the hard work of reconciliation.

There is a huge spiritual danger and consequence for those of us who follow Jesus if we abandon our call to care for the needy. The call to love our neighbor as ourselves cannot be fulfilled if the poor no longer live near us and therefore can't worship with us. In America the poor have been disenfranchised and physically separated from those who could meet their needs, leaving only the government to intervene while the church tends to the elites. Furthermore, when the government does intervene, we demonize those communities as lazy and dependent. We don't have the lens to see how this crisis could be avoided if the church did her part and took care of orphans and widows herself. What would happen if the fierce convictions of Western Christians to save the world were redirected toward loving their neighbor as themselves and seeking justice against systems like redlining?

Although it makes no sense for one group to seek philanthropic achievement around the world while remaining oblivious to the needs right around the corner, it happens. I hate that mission trips are used as a counterfeit to the work of restoration God desires to do in our own communities.

These neglected practices of loving your neighbor come to mind when I hear people say they feel called to help the needy across the globe. The irony is that because they were not trained to listen to the needs of those who have needs at home, they lack the self-awareness to meet true needs presented on mission trips. For example, generous donors with good intentions would offer to build a swimming pool for an orphanage, thinking the kids would love to swim, only to find out the pool had never been used since the day they left. Why? Because the kids didn't know how to swim, the orphanage had no money to maintain the pool, it was a safety issue for the kids, and so on. Instead of leading with questions, we see over and over again that leading with our ideas forces them on communities who don't have the capacity to deny us from doing "good." If not used wisely, with humility and discernment, our money becomes the tool that can further marginalize communities that are already on the margins. The reason we should build bridges within our communities and right the wrongs of systemic racism is so that we can follow God's command to love our neighbors like ourselves.

Dismantling the power hierarchy that's based on the melanin in someone's skin is the work of restorative justice that God desires from his children. Black and Brown people have been made to hold down the bottom of the scale so that capitalism can benefit white supremacy and perpetuate economic disparity. We cannot turn a blind eye to what we see around us locally and globally. Our hearts cannot be callous like that of the priest and Levite we see in the parable of the Good Samaritan in Luke 10:30-35. Although we expect them to naturally be the ones to care for the man who was robbed, beaten, and left to die, the one who comes to the rescue is the Samaritan. He not only takes care of the injured man but makes sure the innkeeper watches over him at the Samaritan's expense. We must ask ourselves who we are in this story. If we are walking past what we know to be unjust because our affiliations frown on us standing for justice, then we are with the priest and Levite of Jesus' time.

If Christians don't have a justice-seeking mindset as they try to meet needs, they will only be discouraged as they encounter resistance to their generosity from those who are tired of being oppressed by them. You know the saying, "People know when you hate them, so either repent or leave them alone"? We shouldn't be surprised when we are not welcomed with open arms as we attempt to "serve" a community that is systematically being oppressed by our own political affiliations.

By institutionalizing generosity, Western philanthropy has institutionalized the gospel itself, preventing each individual believer from going wherever the Lord calls them to go and giving to whomever the Lord calls them to give to. We all have something to offer because we are made in God's image. We must break free of the imprisonment of an institutionalized gospel that restricts us from obeying God and practice hospitality and generosity, which are opposite sides of the same coin. If the Western church would turn her eyes from charity to discipleship, she would break free from the power of money that has her bowing to the agenda of donors rather than those she's called to serve. May we be free from prioritizing institutional mission over God's mission for all his children and freely and relationally display generosity with our time and wealth.

SEVEN

RESTORATIVE JUSTICE

Learn to do what is good.
Pursue justice.
Correct the oppressor.
Defend the rights of the fatherless.
Plead the widow's cause.

ISAIAH 1:17

AS WE EQUIP OURSELVES to seek justice, we should not neglect places like Africa, South Asia, and the Middle East where most Black and Brown people live. Colonialism hasn't stopped; it's just gotten a facelift. Instead of physically enslaving Black and Brown people, it has shifted its focus to economic enslavement, which keeps people of color around the world under its thumb. For example, all of Africa might technically be considered postcolonial, but it's still under the economic and political neocolonialism of the West.

It's almost unheard of to see missional movements challenging big issues such as neocolonization and proxy wars.

It's like our efforts to share the gospel with individuals around the globe are disassociated from their lived existence within an oppressive ecosystem. Most of these disparities would in fact be avoidable if African governments had total autonomy to implement justice-driven policies and practices that benefited their people. South Africa is a great example. While most churches participated in apartheid, others remained silent amplifying the church's complicity. Although some churches opened up their podiums to stand against racism, it wasn't the case for many others.

In 1964 Nelson Mandela addressed the Pretoria Supreme Court, stating, "All whites undergo compulsory military training, but no such training was given to Africans. It was in our view essential to build up a nucleus of trained men who would be able to provide the leadership which would be required if guerrilla warfare started. We had to prepare for such a situation before it became too late to make proper preparations. It was also necessary to build up a nucleus of men trained in civil administration and other professions, so that Africans would be equipped to participate in the government of this country as soon as they were allowed to do so."[1] For South Africans there was no lack of motivation to be self-sustaining and lead in their own country, but their independence was and continues to be a threat to their colonizers.

Western foreign policy as a whole still plays a big part in suppressing Africa's economy and gives no room for Africa's leaders to keep their people's interest first. In fact, US ambassador to the United Nations Linda Thomas-Greenfield admits this reality by stating, "Our policy to the continent is prescriptive. We tell Africans what they should be doing, what they should focus on and what to prioritize. We have taken from but have not given back to Africa."[2] Africa as a whole is of great strategic economic and political interest to the West, and foreign policies toward it are designed to keep the interests of the West elevated and not to benefit Africans.

Unfortunately mission efforts in Africa also do not have a strategy that benefits African pastors and community leaders. They do not address systemic issues but import solutions rather than empowering local leaders to create and implement their own. The lack of awareness of mission trips that go to "help" in war zones after the countries have been destabilized by Western governments is mind-blowing. Because the Western church is not engaged in restorative justice, she fails to recognize that she's just the cleanup crew for the mess her government creates instead of a change agent that stands against destruction in the first place. As the Global South suffers from an aristocratic approach to foreign policy, its church suffers with it. In order to serve the body of Christ around the world, we have to have a framework that supports global justice. It's a complex issue and one that doesn't guarantee any political party a significant alliance.

In her book *Dead Aid*, Zambian economist Dambisa Moyo argues that Western aid is a weapon used to destroy African democracy and prevent Africans from achieving economic independence and standing on their own two feet. Moyo does a beautiful job of explaining how in a democracy an individual's power lies in their ability to use their voice to vote for a government system that looks out for their well-being. Americans vote for a Republican or Democrat based on their personal convictions and what they believe would benefit their families' financial and moral values. Africans, too, should be able to use their votes to secure a future that benefits them. But African individual and collective voices are powerless when it comes to demanding change from their governments because of the loophole created by Western aid. Government officials receive access to free aid without accountability to the people they should be working for, and there are no consequences when they do not deliver on their promises. If they have nothing to prove to the people, why would they work hard to earn their vote? The West funds corrupt governments and takes away the power of individuals, leaving countries in economic disarray.[3] Moyo's point of view is resisted by the West but embraced by most Africans and believed to be the key to ending large-scale poverty on the continent.

When it comes to destabilizing democratic countries on the continent, dead aid is a weapon to pacify the people's anger toward injustice. As long as you keep giving them fish for a day, they won't need to learn how to fish and become self-sufficient. The people's curiosity for a free and decolonized Africa is quickly dampened by threats of war or being made an example of. This is modern-day colonialism, controlling the continent's economy through aid and "good intentions," and the Western church is no small partner in this. If the Western church wants to restore what's been broken, not only is she to stop sending people on poverty tourism disguised as short-term mission, but she must also contribute to the rebuilding of wealth and financial independence in the communities she enters. That is justice, that is accountability, and that is true philanthropy.

Rwanda's president Paul Kagame puts it this way: "Aid is about supporting social and economic transformation that would eventually see people have no need of aid."[4] The type of aid uncorrupted leaders of the continent desire is aid that will help them get their people out of perpetual poverty so they can stand on their own two feet. The type of aid they need is political freedom from Western strategic interest in keeping Russia and China at bay. Africa is of particular interest because it provides natural resources to sustain the West while it's strategically placed to be on guard from potential enemies. The poverty of Africa is not of material resources but dependency on white saviorism, which is suffocating the life out of God's people. If you believe Africa is poor, think again:

> From Algerian petroleum and natural gas in the north, to Zambian copper in the south, these exports dominate many national economies. In Morocco, Tunisia and Lesotho, clothing, shoes and textiles are the biggest exports. Equally, cotton is vital to the economies of Mali, Togo and Benin. In the south and central regions, precious metals and minerals are the biggest exports. This includes gold in Tanzania and South Africa, diamonds in Namibia and the Democratic Republic of the Congo and platinum in Zimbabwe.[5]

There is no lack of raw materials and natural resources in Africa; in fact, the continent is one of the largest suppliers to the world's economy. Yet Africans are the poorest people group in the world. They are not able to use their own God-given natural resources to support and grow their economies; instead their natural resources continue to be extracted and used to supply what the West needs to maintain its economic supremacy.

Engaging in restorative justice means engaging the truth about issues that come from political destruction imposed by Western powers around the globe. Corrupt governments are allowed to remain in power even though people vote them out. The West intervenes when Africans reject its handpicked puppet leaders. If in fact there is true interest in seeking justice and speaking for the voiceless, one must hear the truth Africans want to communicate to the West. Christian leaders who are not equipped to understand the social and economic desires of Africans have no place in leading ministry on the continent that promotes further oppression.

TRUTH AND JUSTICE

Korean American pastor K. Kale Yu describes current social justice phenomena such as Black Lives Matter and the so-called cancel culture as "a secular attempt to purify society." He says, "When the church fails to demand that people confess their sin of racism, God uses secular culture to demand the same."[6] Where the early church felt a direct responsibility to condemn collective sin, the modern church plagued by individualism continues to hide from the path of repentance and reconciliation. If the church is not seeking truth and correcting oppression, the world will continue to do it. The cry for justice will come from anywhere—"I tell you, if they were to keep silent, the stones would cry out" (Luke 19:40)—because it is a cry of truth that God wants to hear and resolve.

It would be irresponsible to assume that we can do true gospel work without engaging in the work of restorative justice. Organizations such as the AND Campaign do a wonderful job of bringing the ideas of gospel and justice together. They state, "Part of God's plan for justice is that those who know Him would seek justice in and with their lives. This is not an extracurricular to the Christian life, but at its core. Any theology or ideology that minimizes or denies the importance of justice in social context is unbiblical and must be rejected as such. . . . The truth and authority of Scripture makes the pursuit of justice for our neighbors a mandatory part of the Christian life."[7]

This tension is what's needed in the Western believer's heart, yet white Christians who want to jump in with good intentions must recognize the need to lead with listening. The question we want to answer is, How can a white Christian be a part of restorative justice without causing unintended harm? Without proper self-awareness, this work is difficult and can in fact excite someone with limited knowledge and qualifications to believe they have authority to speak on the nuances of Black and Brown people's existence. In his book *White Awake*, Daniel Hill discusses how awakening to his whiteness demanded change in the way he lived his life and pursued pastoral ministry:

> There's no crisp way to summarize all I learned during that self-assessment. I was awakening to a reality that had always been there, hidden in plain sight, but I finally had the eyes to see it:
> - My closest friends were white.
> - My most trusted mentors were white.

- The teachers and theologians shaping me were white.
- The authors planting new ideas in my mind were white.
- The church I worked at was white.

Just like all moments of genuine awakening, the discovery was both liberating and terrifying: liberating in the way truth always is, lifting you out of the fog and into the light, and terrifying because this revelation of truth demanded changes.[8]

Hill's self-discovery helped him own his responsibility to the collective community around him as a human being and as a believer. If more white Christians were to undergo the type of self-examination Hill describes, the mission movement would be one marked by truth and justice, attracting the world to Christ.

An identity of unchecked white saviorism in Western missions translates itself into superiority when white missionaries interact with local leaders. It lends itself to pioneerism and centering oneself in the story of God and his people. These leaders completely ignore God's work in local communities prior to their arrival and how it will stay intact long after they're gone.

Faith-based and non-faith-based organizations alike often try to offer solutions to problems they think local communities have, based on their cultural framework looking in to a community as an outsider. Good intentions that are not compatible with local customs create not only mental dependency but also a sense of disdain for local culture and leadership. For example, Western aid organizations have long championed accessibility to birth control for African mothers. African leaders push back on this idea because they don't believe it to be a necessity in their people's context. Obianuju Ekeocha, a Nigerian biomedical scientist and founder and president of Culture of Life Africa, a pro-life activist organization, believes African culture lends itself to the village raising its own children. She points out the lack of aid to invest in the education of children and mothers but the acute interest of the West to impose contraceptives. In an open letter to Melinda Gates, she writes:

> Growing up in a remote town in Africa, I have always known that a new life is welcomed with much mirth and joy. In fact we have a special "clarion" call (or song) in our village reserved for births and another special one for marriages.
>
> The first day of every baby's life is celebrated by the entire village with dancing (real dancing!) and clapping and singing—a sort of "Gloria in excelsis Deo."
>
> All I can say with certainty is that we, as a society, LOVE and welcome babies.
>
> With all the challenges and difficulties of Africa, people complain and lament their problems openly. I have grown up in this environment and I have heard women (just as much as men) complain about all sorts of things. But I have NEVER heard a woman complain about her baby (born or unborn).
>
> Even with substandard medical care in most places, women are valiant in pregnancy. And once the baby

arrives, they gracefully and heroically rise into the maternal mode. . . .

Amidst all our African afflictions and difficulties, amidst all the socioeconomic and political instabilities, our babies are always a firm symbol of hope, a promise of life, a reason to strive for the legacy of a bright future.[9]

I agree with Ekeocha. Most African countries do not have an ultrasexualized culture; there is a sense of communal responsibility that forces children to be birthed within a marriage and raised by a plethora of family members. The overflow of aid that's being forced down the throats of communities in the form of activism for contraceptives is an alarming danger to the continent's pro-life values. This funding is meant to further an agenda that goes against the cultural values of the community and introduce a Western problem where there is none. Just because a Westerner decided an African woman shouldn't have many children, it doesn't mean she shouldn't. Where is the fierce conviction of the Western church for the unborn when it comes to African children?

The West's interest in Africa and other countries in the Global South is not only political and financial but intellectual as well. The diversity visa is one of the tools the United States has used to recruit young, healthy, and educated individuals from the Global South since 1990. The West is a beneficiary of the "brain drain" from the Global South and engages in destabilizing economies so that those who can leave their home looking for a better life would benefit their economy. We hardly ever talk about this in our Christian circles when we discuss immigration:

Emigration rates of high-skilled workers exceed those of low-skill workers in virtually all countries. The skill bias in emigration rates is particularly pronounced in low-income countries. The largest brain drain rates are observed in small, poor countries in the tropics, and they rose over the 1990s. The worst-affected countries see more than 80% of their "brains" emigrating abroad, such as for Haiti, Jamaica, and several small states with fewer than one million workers. About 20 other countries are losing between one-third and one-half of their college graduates. Most are in sub-Saharan Africa (such as Liberia, Sierra Leone, and Somalia) or Asia (such as Afghanistan and Cambodia).[10]

It would be foolish to assume that people leave their home countries because they prefer to live as a minority and second-class citizen in another culture. No, they are forced to leave their homes because of war and economic instability. If they leave for work, they want to be well-compensated for their knowledge and skills in a way the underperforming economy of their country isn't able to provide. As a member of the diaspora community myself, I understand that one of the biggest hindrances to going back home is the fact that we would not be able to live the life we can in the United States. Even so, many of us desire to return to our home countries and give back to our communities. It's clear that the diaspora community represents the best of their countries, but until those countries are able to guarantee a lifestyle that sustains these families, many choose self-exile for the sake of securing a bright future for their children.

The Western church has a unique opportunity to rewrite her legacy by being the driver of reversing the brain drain around the world. One way to do this is to create avenues "for the same educated, talented, promising graduates, entrepreneurs, and professionals to contribute to the prosperity of their countries of origin. A contrasting phenomenon is 'reverse brain drain,' which involves the movement of sending educated, skilled migrants back to their homelands."[11] Think about it. About 65 percent of immigrants to the United States are Christians, so reversing the brain drain would also reverse the exodus of Christians from their home countries and put them back to minister in their own contexts. They would be able to live in their own communities but also serve their people as leaders in the areas they've been trained in. Western charity has created a deep, dark hole in the economies of growing countries that keeps them in a perpetual cycle of poverty. I propose a different approach: to do the things that are proven to be helpful, sending the Nehemiahs of the world back to their homes to restore the wall God has given them insight to rebuild.

SENDING NEHEMIAHS

A friend once told me that one of her greatest fears—one that has prevented her from fully surrendering her life to Christ— was the fear of having to "move to Africa." In her mind a fully surrendered life with Christ meant he would send her to a place where she didn't want to go. I was obviously dumbfounded that she told me her greatest fear was going to the place where I grew up and would do anything to return to. But what I took from that conversation was that she associated surrender with misery. The type of surrender she's heard about in her spiritual journey didn't mean a life of fulfillment she got to experience with Christ but one filled with sorrow and poverty. To her a missionary was one who braved those conditions and lived trying to please God by serving "lost people" despite their misery.

I don't blame my friend one bit. She was a product of a toxic church culture that elevated short-term mission trips where she was exposed to people's pain and vulnerability without earning the right to do so. She didn't have the maturity or spiritual guidance to see them as people who were fully content in their conditions. Her experience further alienated her from connecting to their human experience with vulnerability. It was not the right approach to planting seeds of mission in her heart.

The question now is, How does the Western church help God's children discover a mission that's worth abandoning everything for? There is in fact a joy that comes from being in community with people from all walks of life. Luckily for my friend, joy in our surrender and fullness of God's goodness is what the gospel promises to all believers. If the church is to enlist a volunteer army willing to go anywhere and die for the cause, it must find leaders who want to identify with the suffering of Christ rather than those praying, "I don't want to go." One of the most loving things to do is step away from something we want when we know our engagement will no longer serve the cause, and might even damage it. It's time for the West to step away and participate in facilitating a path for diaspora Christians to lead the way.

There is a unique but harmful privilege built into Western mission work: believers have permission to categorize themselves and others as givers/senders, goers/missionaries, and receivers/the poor. These terms are dangerously segregated and don't allow space for a believer to be all of the above at the same time, experiencing the complex journey of faith God carves out for the surrendered believer. Jesus could identify with all of the above at every moment of his life. Even though he was born a king he had to flee to Egypt as a refugee. While he was a healer he was wounded and died at the cross. While being the giver of all things, he received provisions from people wherever he went, including two fish and five loaves of bread from a little boy. He was everything to all people and died to save us all.

So how does this affect us as believers wrapped in our First-World problems and struggling to become Christians who honor the Lord and carry the mission he gave us? I believe the first step is embracing the prompting of the Holy Spirit to help us step outside our comfortable social bubbles and engage with those who are in the margins. We, too, can live in a nuanced world that allows us not only to be givers but also receivers of love, community, and healing.

Current definitions of godlessness lean too much into physical poverty and not enough into the spiritual. We have to disassociate from the idea that living in the margins means living without God. The mystery of Jesus' birth became something to behold when the three wise men traveled a long distance to see him, a king born in a manger. We forget that the king still resides in the places where the unwise would not go looking for him, in the "ghettos," "slums," "the hood," and "the projects." We can be effective in recognizing God's work globally only if we see him through the eyes of those who live on the margins in our own communities. The Holy Spirit alone in his power and leading can empower and equip us to go where we are needed to do justice, walk humbly, and love mercy (Micah 6:8). If that call draws us to the ends of the earth, that's wonderful, but if it demands we stay at home, we must seek justice where we are. If we truly desire to do God's work, there is plenty to do within the borders of the United States. There are disenfranchised people all around us— immigrants, refugees, and Dreamers who are part of the body of Christ but are not accepted as equal members of our churches.

Even though the majority of immigrants to the United States are Christians, the stereotype is that immigrants are godless. The media has played its part, painting Mexicans as rapists and Arabs as terrorists. When the church doesn't address these issues, which break God's heart, it leaves the door open for us to act on our biased views. The exclusion of people of color from church-planting networks and mission movements didn't happen by accident. We are largely divided by design and don't view each other as family.

I remember the first time someone called me an immigrant. I felt somehow less-than because of the way he said it. Even though Webster's Dictionary defines *immigrant* as "a person who comes to a country to take up permanent residence," this young man's disassociation of himself from me taught me that it meant more than that. It felt like a code word for a freeloader, someone who takes Americans' jobs, someone who cheats their way through life. It's safe to say, it was effective in making me feel othered. If our churches remain segregated, continuing in our limited perspectives, we remain ineffective in our efforts to be a part of the global mission movement.

God had a strategic reason for choosing Nehemiah to go to Jerusalem and mobilize his people to rebuild the city wall. Nehemiah was what Bryan Loritts calls a "culture C," an insider-outsider with better connections and a broader perspective for nuance. People like Nehemiah are immersed in both their home culture and the culture of the land of their exile. With such unique abilities they can use both experiences to create a beautiful middle ground to benefit both cultures. Members of the diaspora community who have been educated in the West and are living their lives as minorities possess a unique ability to walk that fine line of cultural sensitivity and dignity. Not only are they equipped to serve their people in the land of their exile but they also have the trust and often an open invitation to lead in their home of origin. When we look at Nehemiah's strategy in mobilizing God's people to rebuild the wall, we notice that he did it in a way that led them to repentance.

Nehemiah 9 is a beautiful display of remorseful repentance by the Israelites and God's continuous forgiveness of them. If God's mission was simply to rebuild the wall, he could have sent anyone, including the king. With a simple decree from the king the wall would have been built, but then it would have gone to ruins again because the people would not have turned toward God themselves. The wall was a physical indicator of how their hearts had forgotten God. God in his kindness chose a man with no political or financial power but with the right position to appeal to his people and leverage his connections for good. Therefore, as they restored the wall, God restored their hearts through the leadership of Nehemiah.

We see great characteristics of leadership displayed in how Nehemiah quietly and strategically identified the right people for the job. Language was not an issue, nor was cultural understanding. That allowed him to be savvy in adhering to social norms and even outdoing those who tried to intimidate him. He caught the attention of each tribe as he shared God's call to rebuild the wall and gave them the responsibility to build only what was in front of their own homes. He delegated the right thing to the right people in the most attainable manner. The chance to mess it up was low. They all wanted to protect their homes and secure their territories, so they worked hard. Once they started building, the wall that had been sitting in ruin for years and was a source of shame for God's people was rebuilt within fifty-two days. It was not only convenient for each tribe to build the wall that was near their home, but it was genius for long-term upkeep and maintenance. For the sake of their own safety and accountability, each tribe would maintain the wall and worship God while doing so.

How many mission trips have you been on where you ended up repainting a school some other team had painted the year before? How many wells have you dug that were closed off by the time you went back to visit? Most of the time we fail to see the dignity of the people we want to serve and disrespect them by not inviting them to own and lead the good things we champion to them. Nehemiah cared enough about the dignity of his people that even when he provided an answer to their prayers, he used a strategy that was dignifying and sustainable in the long run. The West's missional strategies are largely void of dignity and sustainability because we have been stamped by the transactional legacy left before us. God calls us to build a relational legacy that will outlast generations and bring people to their knees because the relationship leads them to see the true God who desires to commune with them. The question is not what strategy should we implement, but who does God want to send? Who are the people that are strategically best-positioned and whose characters cry out, "Send me, Lord!" (Isaiah 6:8)? It's time to collaborate with the Nehemiahs of our communities and send them off with a blessing.

COLLABORATION

The technology field is one of the fastest-growing and most quickly changing industries because of the collaborative nature of the work. In 2001, seventeen industry leaders came together and wrote the Agile Manifesto, which changed the trajectory of the industry for good. Before the Agile Manifesto the tech industry used a project management method called the "waterfall," which was an old-fashioned, top-down strategy: "You make a big plan upfront and then execute in a linear fashion, hoping there won't be any changes in the plan."[12] This method was not intentionally designed for the tech industry but was adapted from manufacturing and construction. Its downfall was that there was no room for iteration, and once a product was built no one knew its deficiencies until after it reached the consumer's hands. But with the fast-changing nature of the software industry, there needed to be a more nimble method of managing projects for teams to be effective—hence the Agile Manifesto. The manifesto explains the need for "individuals and interactions over processes and tools, working software over comprehensive documentation, customer collaboration over contract negotiation, responding to change over following a plan."[13] This helped the tech industry know how to prioritize and make its next major moves.

New roles were necessary to carry out proper project management. The realization was that if people who preferred to spend time going over processes, creating documentation, and following a specific plan were instructing people to do what was the opposite of their gifting, the manifesto wouldn't succeed. Therefore, there was freedom to create new roles that would bring on project managers to ensure individuals were interacting fluidly while the software was being built. Customers became part of the process of designing and building by giving feedback, and teams would respond by making changes. This essentially required someone to actively create a communicative environment and give the experts room to do what they did best. This role was called a "scrum master," someone who facilitates communication and collaboration between leaders and team members to ensure a successful outcome. And today the tech industry is booming; it is not only the fastest growing but also the highest paying industry, attracting more people to join it.

In a similar way, there is a need in the Western mission movement to revitalize our manifesto by adhering to the Word of God, enabling servant leaders who cry out to the Lord, "Send me!" I believe we should prioritize contextualizing our approach to the culture, language, and customs of the people over our own missional statements and five-year goals. We should focus on identifying and supporting Nehemiahs who are burdened for their people and are ready to go rather than recruiting and convincing people why they should go. We should seek to provide solutions to existing problems communities are trying to solve rather than providing a Western solution to problems that don't exist in their context. We should be able to measure success based on the metrics available in the community and give them the power to grow the way they see fit rather than forcing them to apply Western benchmarks and standards that suffocate.

The role of the Western church in this season of change for global missions is largely to be the ear that listens. The ability to create safe spaces for Global South leaders to sit at the same table as their Western counterparts determines her success. Allowing them to strategize and collaborate on a regular basis so that their work for kingdom change would have a cohesive path would change the game. Understanding what made the tech industry what it is today can help us to dare to reimagine a new form of mission. No longer should we be comfortable in our old method of giving money so others can go. We must focus on where the real money is: identifying Nehemiahs and sending them back home with the people they need to succeed. God can give us a new passion for reframing mission for the next generation, the individuals he wants to use to rebuild the broken walls of his church. Empowered by the Holy Spirit, these warriors for the kingdom delight in their suffering, seeking out restorative justice and revolutionizing the mission movement. We must carve a path for training and developing the new generation of Christian leaders to become listeners, collaborators, and servant leaders. It's my prayer that more leaders rise up and claim their call to rebuild their territory so God's work will not be neglected.

EIGHT

THE FUTURE OF MISSION

*Within a few decades, Christianity will be overwhelmingly
a non-European, non-white religion. What we are seeing is
no less than the creation of a new Christendom, which, for
better or worse, will play a major role in world affairs.*

PHILIP JENKINS

I SHARED MY STORY of immigration during a women's
conference once, and two Latina women came to talk to me
during the break. One was crying and speaking in Spanish,
and her friend was translating while holding her hands. She
said, "Thank you! For the first time at my church, I felt like
my story was being shared and that God was telling me that
he sees me, that I am not an outcast in this country, that he
has a place for me in his household, and that one day I will
tell my testimony as you have shared yours today." She was
hopeful to have seen another Brown woman on stage boldly
speaking about God's purpose on a matter that the church
deemed shameful: the immigration journey.

That weekend at the conference God taught me many things, but that specific encounter tugs at my heart because I, too, used to cry when someone mentioned Ethiopia from stage or shared their immigration story. I know that feeling. I know what it means for my story to be represented in the house of the Lord—it means that I, too, am part of the body. The desire to have a voice kept me from leaving the majority white evangelical church for a long time. Even after realizing my leadership would never be deemed sufficient, I stayed in hopes that others who shared my experiences would find encouragement from someone like me in a leadership role at their church. I wanted to be there for the one girl who might need to see someone who looked like her. I wanted her to know God saw her.

Unfortunately most Black and Brown people in this country have more unpleasant experiences to share than stories of welcome and understanding. In the last five years we have seen high-profile companies like Starbucks, Airbnb, Google, and Uber make appearances in the news after the revelation of racially insensitive and overtly prejudiced policies. These organizations have drawn public attention because of horrifying experiences endured by people of color. The good news is that things are changing, and inclusion and equity are being incorporated in the hiring process for many secular organizations. What bothers me is the fact that the secular world is ten steps ahead of our churches. When we struggle to believe each other's experiences and stories, we weaken the power of our testimony and become less and less relevant to a generation that is seeking to find refuge from evil.

INTIMIDATING BUT WORTH IT

The early church made a way for those on the margins and created a safe haven where they could worship God without hindrance. The opposite is happening in the United States, where standing up for those on the margins is seen as a sinful act instead of a righteous one. The evangelical church of America has been in the news for resisting diversity and inclusion, which is a horrible way to be known by the world. Russell Moore, president of the Ethics and Religious Liberty Commission of the Southern Baptist Convention—the largest Protestant denomination in the United States—recently exited the organization with a letter that shook it to its foundation. *The Atlantic* reports:

> His departure was not primarily prompted, as many people had assumed, by his role as an outspoken critic of Donald Trump, although that had clearly upset powerful members within the politically and theologically conservative denomination. Instead, the letter suggests, the breach was caused by the stands he had taken against sexual abuse within the SBC and on racial reconciliation, which had infuriated the executive committee.[1]

Dr. Moore is just one example of the many leaders who are taking a stance. Beth Moore, a women's Bible teacher and advocate for sexual abuse survivors, has made her voice loud and clear in speaking publicly against racism, and she, too, has ended her relationship with the Southern Baptist Convention. Megachurches such as McLean Bible Church are facing internal dissension that has divided the congregation and prevented the election of elders from taking place because senior leaders like David Platt are being accused of teaching critical race theory.

This is making the front pages of newspapers and websites, and it's happening to those the white evangelical church once revered as its most trusted and beloved leaders. Unfortunately their voices are welcomed only within a boundary. When they start teaching on the collective historical sin of the church, they are shunned or pushed out as nonviable witnesses of the gospel. This movement of publicly shaming leaders who dare challenge white supremacy mirrors old practices of lynching Black slaves who dared run away for their freedom. These public lynchings were intended to make an example of those slaves so that if anyone else dared to pursue truth, freedom, or joy, they would face the same punishment. This is a tactic of intimidation the enemy uses to scare God's people, just like Jezebel did with God's prophets in 1 Kings:

> Ahab told Jezebel everything that Elijah had done and how he had killed all the prophets with the sword. So Jezebel sent a messenger to Elijah, saying, "May the gods punish me and do so severely if I don't make your life like the life of one of them by this time tomorrow!"
>
> Then Elijah became afraid and immediately ran for his life. When he came to Beer-sheba that belonged to Judah, he left his servant there, but he went on a day's journey into the wilderness. He sat down under a broom tree and prayed that he might die. He said, "I have had enough! Lord, take my life, for I'm no better than my ancestors." Then he lay down and slept under the broom tree. (1 Kings 19:1-5)

We know how the story ends—God renews Elijah's strength and he finds the courage to stand up to evil and destroy it. There is a price believers must pay for standing up for truth and serving as God's prophets at a time such as this one. God's desire for his church is for justice, mercy, and peace, and this is not something we can achieve by sitting around and talking about it. There is a price, and it might cost us things we never thought we'd have to give up: our careers, our circles of friends, our finances, and the affiliations that have made our lives easier. Diversity comes at a cost, but it is a cost worth paying because it is the sacrifice we must make to beautify the bride of Christ and present her as blameless to the coming king.

Lamin Sanneh, a Gambian who was professor of missions and world Christianity at Yale Divinity School, had this to say about the diversity and mission of the early church:

> If Christianity was born out of mission, then it was in mission the end of history as people knew it happened—the end of the dogmatic culture, the end of religion as patriotic entitlement. It was the last time that the center would hold the world. What the Romans knew as the center, now was a new form of human identity and understanding. It was in mission that the church was known as a diverse cultural and historical event. From the experience and example of the disciples, mission became a bigger multicultural pluralism movement. In a matter of a century the mission took Christianity into diverse worlds.[2]

What a beautiful picture to remind us that this struggle of racial justice might just be God's way of bringing revival to the West and allowing the emergence of multiethnic churches we have been praying for and need.

Where else should we collectively lament the injustices of our days other than the house of God? It makes perfect sense to me that those who desire to make God's house a place of truth and justice are the ones being persecuted. The enemy actively uses tactics of division and distrust to diminish the light given to the body of Christ to shine for a world darkened by injustice. Those who have been pushed out for seeking justice are collectively ready for a church community that glorifies Christ in her expression of the diversity his kingdom represents. America as a representation of multiculturalism and globalization is the perfect place for the body of Christ to experience true diversity as described in Revelation 7:9-10:

> After this I looked, and there was a vast multitude from every nation, tribe, people, and language, which no one could number, standing before the throne and before the Lamb. They were clothed in white robes with palm branches in their hands. And they cried out in a loud voice:
>
> Salvation belongs to our God,
> who is seated on the throne,
> and to the Lamb!

How amazing would it be for God's church to reflect the diversity of this beautiful country we live in? How much richer and stronger would our knowledge of God become if we gleaned such diverse theological perspectives? How brilliant would our kids' lives be if they experienced other cultures in their interactions with close friends? The next generation of missional leaders would naturally grow up in multicultural churches and be ready to carry the gospel effectively around the globe. We would have access to an army of culturally fluid and equipped believers who would be ready not only to be sent out but also to be invited into cultures that feel dignified by their presence.

The lack of diversity in evangelical churches and mission organizations cannot be overlooked if we are to reimagine mission and discuss the future of Western mission. The movement must outperform its past legacy, which has left out the voices from the majority of the world. There is a sense of frustration in people of color at the slow pace of change well-intentioned white evangelicals desire to see. The problem is that desire itself without intentional systemic and organizational change cannot produce the intended outcome. Pursuing a strategy of "diversity hires" who affirm the same theology, play the same music style, and fit in the evangelical bubble comfortably won't bring the desired change. We must consider a deeply revitalized approach to the future of mission that not only includes but also centers the voices of global leaders.

INCLUSIVE MISSIONAL APPROACH

Besides addressing the lack of equity and inclusion in mission organization leadership, I focus in my consulting work on helping Western Christians engage leaders of the diaspora community. I believe these diaspora leaders are perfectly suited to accomplish the work God has called the church to do in reaching the world with the gospel. If you take a look at the "About Us" section of almost any mission organization, you will see mostly one demographic on the leadership team. I'm always baffled to see that leaders of initiatives for Africa,

Latin America, and Asia are mostly white people. One must wonder if there is a lack of qualified individuals from those continents or if the problem is in fact systemic. The idea that there aren't qualified evangelical leaders around the world gives us an excuse not to try to find them. The reality is that there are more than enough qualified leaders, but they don't necessarily fit Western organizations' theological, strategic, and cultural lenses. What these organizations really want is to find people with the same culture but who have a different color on the outside. Black and Brown people who adhere to their norms rise to leadership positions quickly, but there aren't many who have managed to hold on to their culture and advance to the top. This is the wrong approach to making change in an increasingly diverse country where Christianity is expressed in so many unique ways.

It's still hard for me to fathom the lack of diversity in the leadership makeup of global mission organizations in this day and age. Those that claim to have a "heart for the nations" exclude the nations from their tables. The growing number of Christians among the diaspora community all around the world need to lead the way, because they hold the key to a strategic and beautiful reimagining of mission. It's time for us to ask critical questions as we teeter on the precipice of the decline of mission in the West.

The key is in our hands, but we must open the doors for leaders from the Global South to truly lead without systemic hindrances. Scripture is full of stories about how God used the journeys of immigrants to make himself known, not only to the sojourners but also to those who came in contact with them. As we have already discussed, Nehemiah was used in mighty ways for God's kingdom, even though he was in exile. God strategically placed him under a powerful king whom he faithfully served until called back home to restore the wall of Jerusalem, and while doing so he restored the faith of God's people. There is much of Nehemiah's journey that mirrors the diaspora movement globally, and closely studying his leadership strategy might be what Western missions needs to course-correct and become part of the work God is already doing around the world.

Nehemiah's story reminds me of the many immigrant churches around the United States that are holding on to a dynamic and bold expression of the gospel message. The missional movement within the diaspora community in the United States and around the globe is not something the Western church has done a good job of acknowledging or learning from. Besides having an international pastor show up once a year for a global mission sermon or celebration of what their church has helped them do, churches aren't requesting these pastors to speak at conferences or teach at seminaries. There is a gap in forming a brotherhood and collective spirit of collaboration between leaders of diaspora churches and white evangelical pastors. "Them versus us" is an undeniable fact—one we must pay attention to and question. While Western missions acknowledges the dynamic spiritual movement of the Global South, it hasn't tapped into the powerful impact God is making around the world through his global church. Although some church planting networks, churches, and mobilizing agencies have started talking about this gap, there is still a tendency to bring a Western solution that doesn't center and elevate the voices of diaspora leaders.

The prayer warriors I encounter in my Christian diaspora community keep me from falling for the idols of Western culture. Their dedication to keeping churches open at all hours for anyone who wants a safe space to escape the brutality of the exiled life is the backbone of our communities. When I was going through my green card process, I would go to the Ethiopian evangelical church near me at six o'clock every morning to pray with fellow believers. I was always accompanied by at least ten people who came to intercede before the Lord in prayer. I marveled at the dedication of the pastors who had been at the church the night before teaching discipleship classes and returned to pray for those in need early in the morning. The aroma of Christ and the beauty of community made me think I was in fact experiencing the spirit of the early church. From phone and Zoom prayer services to telegram and WhatsApp prayer chains, the Christian diaspora community around the world is connected and collectively praying for one another.

My experience with this beautiful Christian love and community is not unique. We hear testimonies from brothers and sisters in the Middle East that God is revealing himself through dreams and visions. Those in Europe or here in the United States share about opportunities God has given them to freely proclaim his name and start Bible studies in their workplaces for the first time in their lives. The cloud of witnesses that surrounds the work God is doing through his diaspora is a thick and tangible experience I wouldn't have survived without. As someone who is part of this movement, I find it difficult to suggest a solution for the future of missions or create a "mission strategy" that doesn't center the experiences of millions of diaspora Christians around the globe. Unless the Western church stops and reframes her approach to global missions, she'll be like a clanging gong that shouts love without truly loving and embracing her own.

In his book *The Celtic Way of Evangelism*, George Hunter shares the story of Saint Patrick, who spent his childhood as a slave in Ireland and by special revelation grew closer to God and found his way back to England, where he pursued priesthood.[3] After being ordained as a bishop he returned to Ireland upon God's calling, which led him to redefine the meaning of evangelism. Even though the British looked down on the Celts as barbarians, Saint Patrick—an insider with a deep understanding of Celtic culture and a love for the people—subversively shared the gospel without dampening the beauty of the culture. In fact the Celts ended up being called "barbarian Christians." This to me is a beautiful approach to evangelization that maintains cultural dignity by allowing space for the people's own cultural expression. The Celts could bring all of themselves as they pursued Christ in their study of Scripture and fellowship in community.

When I first read this book it tugged at my heart and I couldn't put it down until I was finished. I questioned why this book wasn't being used as a staple text for the mission movement. It was telling me my story of one day needing to go back home and spread the Word of God among my people, with whom I identify and whose sin brings deep sorrow to my soul. I can assure you that every diaspora leader I have had the pleasure of meeting will tell you the same thing. They want to go back home and do God's work, and they are deeply invested. Very few will say their calling is to a people group in a foreign land. Most want to take back all the knowledge and experience they gained while following God as an immigrant/exile and invest back into their own people. Not including them in the Western missional movement of today will result in a great loss for the global church.

UNIFIED FOR GOD'S MISSION

Religion News Service reports that "75% of white evangelical Protestant Republicans, the highest percentage of any Republican group, believe immigrants are invading American society. And . . . 68% of white evangelicals believe the United States does not have a responsibility to house refugees—a significantly higher percentage than the national average."[4] This report presents a serious reality we must confront: white evangelicals' anti-immigrant political views violate the biblical mandate to care for strangers and put the Western church in a position of direct participation in the persecution of the vulnerable. This is an area where we need to have a clear stance, because it would be hypocritical to send the very same people who don't want immigrants among them to the homeland of those they despise with the "gospel." We have to be honest with ourselves as we pave a path for the future of the mission. This approach simply doesn't work.

Our segregated worship is costing us the opportunity to do the work God has called us to do. Indeed, the workers are few because only a few are living an integrated life. It's safe to assume that the majority of immigrants who are Christians go to churches planted by immigrant or Black pastors. In fact, in the United Kingdom, "the denominations that are growing—Pentecostal, Evangelical, and other charismatic congregations—can thank black-majority churches that have expanded to serve the flow of immigrants from West, Central, and East Africa."[5] This is another factor that adds to the complexity of segregation by faith in the West. For the sake of language, comfort, and a safe space to worship with people who have experienced a similar life, most first-generation immigrants prefer to worship in nonwhite churches.

There is an advantage to immigrants worshiping together. It helps preserve their culture and language. In fact, we should support these churches and not contribute to further disenfranchising a vulnerable community that has found safety in a land that is not their home. They have a deep sense of need to be together and build a new life in a new land, especially when broken systems place roadblocks on the path to rebuilding their lives. The problem comes when children who culturally identify with both their parents' birth country and their own—in this case America—enter the picture. These kids don't fully fit in to their parents' church and neither do they feel welcomed in white evangelical spaces.

In most cases immigrant churches don't have the ability to spiritually feed two generations of Christians with two cultural expressions of faith. Most international pastors can shepherd the parents sufficiently, but the kids are unintentionally neglected in those churches for lack of cultural connectedness and sometimes even language barriers. Today, churches are emerging that are being planted by second-generation leaders—Asian Americans in particular are doing wonderful work to bridge that gap. If the majority of American churches miss the opportunity to invest in second-generation immigrant kids and the diaspora community as a whole, we will certainly miss the most strategic people God has placed within our reach to partner with.

King Artaxerxes in the book of Nehemiah didn't miss his opportunity to support God's work when he helped Nehemiah. He must have had a close relationship with Nehemiah to be able to detect his sadness, otherwise it would be odd for a king to show concern for his servant's mood: "Why do you look so sad, when you aren't sick? This is nothing but sadness of the heart" (Nehemiah 2:2). All it took was one question from the king for Nehemiah to invite him into God's mission to rebuild the wall of Jerusalem. If a king can show compassion and care for his servant, shouldn't the church of Christ, which is redeemed by his blood, show hospitality for God's own children? Failing to do so will cost her the role God intends her to play in participating in restorative justice. If the white evangelical church doesn't want to be a part of God's movement around the world, God will not force her hand. But woe is she who forfeits her seat at the table of grace.

There are in fact some wonderful efforts being made by evangelical leaders who understand their role in restorative justice. The Evangelical Immigration Table states:

> As evangelical Christians, our approach to immigration policy is driven by biblical principles. We believe that each person is made in God's image and so should be treated humanely; that God has ordained the role of civil government, including the responsibility to protect the safety of citizens, maintain order and respect the rule of law, which is diminished when laws are violated without consequence; that because God created the family unit, governments should not violate the unity of the family

except in the rarest of circumstances; that God is concerned with the wellbeing of those who are vulnerable, including the orphan, the widow and the foreigner, and it is appropriate for citizens to encourage our government to treat these vulnerable groups with fairness and compassion; and that God delights in redemption, when those who have violated the law are able to be restored.[6]

This is a great start and a powerful way to help believers think through the complex reality many of their immigrant brothers and sisters live in. I believe the leading voices in these types of movements must be pastors and leaders of immigrant churches. Their willingness to participate in efforts such as this is key, as they can continue to advocate for their sheep from the unfiltered perspective of the afflicted.

REPRESENTATIVE LEADERSHIP

I have the privilege of knowing and serving with some amazing diaspora leaders. Diaspora believers are the epitome of bridge builders. You may find very few of them in vocational ministry or hired by Western institutions to be "missionaries" per se—most are just living their lives in their communities, working on growing small businesses or pastoring their flocks. They might be going to school while working a job that supports their family here in the States and also back home. These leaders fill the hole that the immigration process has created and stand in the gap for their communities. You find them at court hearings translating, helping college applicants whose parents can't, and assisting at detention centers trying to reconnect children with parents who were separated at the border. They don't fit in the white evangelical space because there is not a neat box to slot them into if they bring all their lived experience and their passion with them. Although they're an asset to the majority white evangelical church and perfect candidates to be church planters, they remain on the outside, resulting in the lack of truly multiethnic churches in the United States.

Immigrant church leaders sit on the outskirts of the greater church body in America because evangelicalism demands assimilation. There is no room for someone who is a fully devoted follower of Christ and wants to remain fully Korean, Chinese, Mexican, Nigerian, Ethiopian, and so on to be recognized as a leader of an evangelical organization or church. In 2020 *Christianity Today* reported that "black clergy heading up multiracial churches have increased from 4 percent to 18 percent from 1998 to 2019. The number of Hispanics with their own church has risen from 3 percent to 7 percent in that time, with Asian Americans increasing from 3 percent to 4 percent."[7] These numbers show a growing and vibrant movement of churches within the diaspora. So why don't we see them leading from a place of authority on mainstream evangelical stages?

In his book *Brown Church*, Robert Chao Romero shares the story of Kari, a Dreamer with undocumented parents. Kari tells of her love for Jesus, whom she found in a land that despises her:

The dream began with my parents, two young warriors, determined to escape a world of poverty in search for a future in a country where rumor had it, dreams came true. They sacrificed everything they held dear so I could carry on with their dreams. America has seen me grow, cry, hurt, laugh, and fight for twenty-four years since I migrated at eight months old from Oaxaca. The sobering truth about what it means to be undocumented in this country wounded my validity and identity. The limitations, persecution of undocumented communities, and the fear of separation from my family pushed me into coping with art, music, and smoking. I held a great grudge against God for years. But in 2012, I received a wonderful gift in this country—the salvation, grace, and love from Jesus Christ. I realize Jesus brought me to this country as a foreigner to understand vulnerability and marginalization to be more like him. When I had to pay $5,000 out-of-pocket to pay for UCLA because undocumented students didn't get financial aid, he provided. He knew my desire to become an educator and made the way with DACA. Now I stand as a kinder/first grade Special Education teacher completely in love with serving the children of this community. My identity and citizenship are found in Christ, and no human law will change this. I rest in his love knowing that he too was despised and rejected but he loves with an unfailing love. My dream and purpose in this country is to be a fountain of his love and grace.[8]

This is the reality of the persecuted children of God who have found their Savior in exile and are living in the beautiful tension of a fully surrendered life that is wrapped in persecution propelling them to sanctification. To those like Kari God says, "Rejoice as you share in the sufferings of Christ, so that you may also rejoice with great joy when his glory is revealed" (1 Peter 4:13).

Every four years Americans fail to put their political agenda aside and act on behalf of the marginalized, people of color, and communities around them who truly need a neighbor. Every four years they miss the opportunity to make their churches a place of refuge and brotherhood, and, importantly, to witness to those on the outskirts waiting to see if there truly is hope in the house of the Lord. God's house turns hostile to those who don't align with the political agenda of the congregation.

The next generation of missional leaders will include people like Kari, living witnesses to the power of the gospel through not only knowledge of theology but a testimony of lived victory in Christ Jesus. With all the resources evangelical churches have to pour into the future of the mission movement, I question why they turn their eyes away from unity in diversity. The people God has called them to unify and commune with are living in the United States. Yet the pull for instant gratification from an act of temporal service on behalf of people who live far away is strong, and the cycle continues. Have you ever asked yourself why you don't hear testimonies such as Kari's on Sunday at your church? Why hardship and persecution are not preached as part of the Christian journey? The lack of stories like hers in our collective worship spaces serves as a painful reminder that God has distanced himself from organized religion that is married to a political party and its pursuit of happiness on earth. We must move to the middle, divorce ourselves from political idolatry, and refuse to support a candidate who doesn't fully stand on a righteous cause.

We must move forward to pave a path for the future of the mission. The mission of God carried out by his disciples birthed the early church, which was multiethnic, horizontally philanthropic, and a threat to Roman power. Our move to a just mission is bound to produce the same result as before, thus we must prepare to count the cost and endure the outcome.

NINE

A REASON TO STAY

Today, if you hear his voice, do not harden your hearts.

HEBREWS 4:7

WHEN THE COVID-19 PANDEMIC brought travel to a halt, it gave us an opportunity to stop and examine our priorities in life. This pause affected the trajectory of most institutions and caused them to rethink their strategies. Some companies found out they were more profitable with their employees working from home and that staff morale was surprisingly high, so they decided to keep working remotely long-term. I think it's safe to assume that we collectively believe we will never go back to a prepandemic normal. Life after the pandemic has brought a new normal, and we are all adjusting.

The church is no exception. The time away from overly produced, experience-centered, and consumeristic church services has taught many of us that we don't need all the bells and whistles to worship God. We were able to worship God in our homes with our families, neighbors, and with the global church around the world through online options, and we were forced to be okay with a stripped-down worship experience. Many have discovered newfound spiritual growth though a close-knit community of believers in the midst of this isolated season of life.

In fact, Barna reports that exactly "one-quarter of practicing Christians (25%), versus 15 percent of all US adults, said they were more satisfied with their mental and emotional well-being during the Covid-19 crisis. Though the data can't speak to the direction of this correlation, practicing Christians, by their own accounts, were more likely to hold steady or see some improvement through the pandemic."[1] While many have walked away from their churches and don't attend any service anymore, the chatter I hear from my Christian friends is that they feel purposeful in their worship now. I believe we've been forced to experience the meaning of Matthew 18:20, that there is no need for more than the gathering of two or more in God's name for his presence to be known. As many of us are embracing our new normal in practicing intentional communal worship with a few loved ones, we also must question what our missional activities should look like.

This is a critical time to fix what's broken in the Western mission movement. One of the biggest issues as discussed in previous chapters is the tendency to label people of color as the problem and white people as the solution. It's not only people of color who struggle with this approach; my white friends are also struggling with this label and actively trying to distance themselves from the negative legacy left them by their ancestors. They no longer want to be the saviors; they want to experience community and mutuality. Together we are trying to go back to what the Bible teaches about discipleship and mission so we can be effective in the work God has called us to do. Now that Covid-19 created a pause in the mass sending of short- and long-term missionaries, we have a great opportunity to discuss solutions that are mutually agreeable. These solutions certainly will not give the instant gratification most Western institutions have been able to manufacture through monolithic cultural practices, but they will be the right ones to build long-term solutions.

UNLEARNING HARMFUL PRACTICES

Sometimes we need to unlearn the old to make space to learn something new: "Truly I tell you, unless a grain of wheat falls to the ground and dies, it remains by itself. But if it dies, it produces a lot of fruit" (John 12:24). The Western mission movement is dependent on taking people on mission trips to expose them to Christian service. These trips have traditionally been seen as a necessary strategy for recruiting future missionaries. Now that they are not an option, it's normal to experience a sense of anxiety and assume the gospel is not being shared.

In 2020 I created an online community, "Just Missions," with the purpose of helping missionaries, receivers of missionaries, and ministry leaders engage with one another on an open platform and discuss the harmful effects of Western missions. The group gives Westerners the chance to hear from the receivers of missions without the financial power dynamic that typically robs them of openly discussing the truth. Through this platform, I receive inquiries from pastors and mission leaders on a regular basis asking, "What do we need to do in the meantime while we wait for the pandemic to be over?" While that's a good question to ask, I challenge the assumption that they'll go back to their old ways as soon as traveling is safe again. My answer is unpopular but one I must share in order to help Western Christians think through their role in the next phase of the missional movement: I believe we should celebrate the inability to travel freely into communities that didn't have the heart or resources to tell us not to come in the first place. I've been in many conversations with local pastors and ministry leaders in my own community, and these individuals have shared with me that they would be grateful if there was a way for Western Christians to help without sending the masses. So I ask, Can we unlearn short-term mission trips as the main way for the mission movement to continue?

In communities that host short-term mission trips, faith leaders have to act as travel agents who "babysit" hundreds of visitors a year, when what they really want is to have the financial support to focus their energy on the work on the ground. Most of the time the tourism industry in their country can fulfill the role imposed on these local leaders, but because of how we've always done short-term missions, we end up becoming one more burden they have to carry. If we stayed back and sent our money along with a few bicultural and bilingual people who could represent us, we wouldn't need to impose on the daily work they are trying to do. I do think there is a time and a place for a church to visit another church across the ocean, but it should be done upon invitation, not by inquiry. When we go to churches to encourage them, we should extend an invitation for them to come visit and encourage us as well. As long as the relationship is one-sided, it will not be equally mutual.

It's not only local leaders who see something wrong with Western mission practices but also missionary kids (MKs) on their journey of racial awakening and reconciliation. One friend who grew up in Asia as an MK told me that she went through the vetting process of one of the largest mission organizations in America. It was the one her parents were a part of because she wanted to follow in their footsteps and become a missionary. She was sure this was what she wanted to do with her life. But as a justice-minded Christian, she was turned off by how her training focused on support raising and keeping the organizational structure intact. What she expressed was that the organization's lack of desire to talk about what was currently affecting American Christianity and how that impacts the global mission movement didn't give her the tools she needed to become a witness in the global space. That forced her to choose to "pause pursuing being a missionary" as she put it.

She said, "It's like they're not impacted by what's happening in America right now. Our brothers and sisters of color are crying out for justice, but we're being trained to keep the status quo intact and go abroad." I loved hearing her story and was encouraged by this God-fearing woman's choice to keep in step with the Spirit and go where he sends her. She didn't pursue her comfort or the status of saviorism that these institutions provide their missionaries. She knew her God was big enough to send her at the right time; till then it was time to stay and wait on the Lord, doing the work he called her to do in her backyard.

People like her are the reason I don't want the Just Missions online community to be a "sending" agency per se but a connector of like-minded believers with local leaders and a champion of diaspora voices and leadership.

As I see it, there is more reason for white Westerners to stay put than there is for them to go to other countries as missionaries. This is especially true for those who have used their privilege to enter environments without considering the consequences of their actions. This is a great time to assess your strategy, support your partners on the ground, and learn from local minority pastors while at home. This is a time to look around and ask, "Who is my neighbor?" It is a great opportunity to build and not force relationships with people who may not be in your regular circle.

DEINSTITUTIONALIZING MISSION

Often I hear indigenous leaders' frustration about how they are confined to roles that are beneath their educational and skill level, while the Westerners leading their organizations have neither the level of education nor the skill set these leaders possess. It's heartbreaking to observe the level of systemic oppression these leaders endure in their own countries at the hands of missionaries who go in the name of "selflessness" but maintain the comfortable lifestyle their American salary offers them in another part of the world. Not only is this unjust, it's damaging to the name of God. I know more than a few individuals who raise money in the name of "mission" but have created financial empires at the locals' expense. For those of us who come from these communities but consider ourselves evangelicals, it puts us in a position where we have to expose the evil done in the name of God. The push to deinstitutionalize mission is not out of spite but because we see the severe damage Western institutions have caused in our communities. In a recent report the *Washington Post* revealed how Margaret Ruto, an ordinary woman from Pennsylvania, discovered that a missionary was abusing children near her family's village in Kenya:

> It was the summer of 2018, and she found the village in uproar. Two girls, 12 and 14, had recently escaped and shared horror stories of sexual abuse at the hands of the orphanage's director, Gregory Dow. Ruto was led to a rumpled patch of earth behind the orphanage. Former employees said a 9-month-old boy buried there had died a few years earlier after choking on something while he'd been left unsupervised. Standing over the grave, she felt dizzy. It was a moment that would divide her life into a before and an after: a transformation from an "ordinary woman" into a detective.[2]

I had the privilege of interviewing Ruto in front of our Just Missions community. She shared how a simple visit back home to Kenya led her to uncover horrific injustice and how God had used these events to change the trajectory of her life—from working as a nurse in Pennsylvania to pursuing criminal justice as her career path. In fact, it is not hard to find headlines such as these. Another one you might have heard of reads, "U.S. Citizen Went to Uganda to Help Kids. Now Her Charity Is Accused of Killing Them." People who testify in these cases give testimonies saying, "I knew she was not trained, but she had this presence about her that you kind of just believed."[3] Similar stories are too numerous to list, but no longer will they stay in darkness. Human rights organizations led by locals and people of the African diaspora like Margaret Ruto, who have access to the FBI in the United States, are demanding legal action against heinous crimes committed by unqualified people under the name of "missionary" and aid workers, who do more harm than good. The Western church has yet to engage these issues transparently, and this lack of accountability speaks to how much of mission is done to benefit the giver without any protection for those hurt in the process. As passionate as it seems to be about missions, the Western church has turned a blind eye to the harm it's causing. Whether it is directly or indirectly, white saviorism under the guise of missions has created an umbrella under which many perform harmful acts to those who trust the system. Secular organizations are looking for solutions, but God's people should be leading the way. We should not miss such an opportunity to truly shine the light of Christ to those we've hurt—to model humility, ask for forgiveness, seek restoration, and be led before we attempt to lead.

This is not only something felt and mourned by those on the receiving end. It won't be fair not to include the concern and frustration of many Western missionaries who are tired of the old transactional approach and want to change it. That's why diaspora leaders and Western leaders who want to see change need a to ideate, collaborate, and implement change without the pressure of a power dynamic that prevents honest and sanctifying conversations from happening. This is why the Just Missions platform exists, to allow these leaders and advocates to interact with one another without any obligation other than authentic relationship. Hearing stories like Ruto's has been the affirmation I need to keep going, to challenge the status quo and develop ways for people who see wrong to speak up and do something about it. When people see a problem but feel helpless to correct it, they either distance themselves from that particular situation or retaliate. We cannot passively watch as the next generation of Christian leaders actively does the work of deconstruction of their faith to the point that they find the mission movement offensive to God and his people. We must step in and shepherd their journey by acknowledging past mistakes and paving the way for forgiveness, reconciliation, and restoration. We should and can help them rethink their beliefs and strategies and empower them to do what they've been called to do for God's kingdom. They can, in fact, walk boldly in their faith, proclaiming Christ the Savior around the globe while actively distancing themselves from the stains of the sins of the past.

As we engage in unlearning and undoing harmful practices, we must confront the reality that this journey will lead us to staying put for a while. Not going anywhere for a mission trip is a tough thing to consider for the Western church. Although there might not be movements of massive mission trips to fill the hole of our summers and spring breaks, that doesn't mean we cannot be effective in our own communities. Choosing to be intentional to finally see people from the Global South who live around us as equals and building authentic relationships with God's image bearers in whatever skin tone they come with will be our next step in reaching the world with the gospel.

For those of us who have the luxury of working from home, in coworking spaces and coffee shops there is a plethora of opportunity to meet people from all walks of life. Although I'm personally not a big fan of chitchatting and refuse to initiate a conversation with a random stranger, I've had amazing friends who have nudged me to step out of my comfort zone. People like my friend Philippe, who sends me a list of at least ten people he's prayed for or shared the gospel with within a single week, keep me on my toes. When the gospel is a fire that burns within our soul, we cannot contain it until we go abroad to share it with "the poor." It bursts out of us as good news should and attracts those who need the good news to us. It is magnetic; it fills our Jerusalem and makes a way for Judea, Samaria, and the ends of the earth to hear it too.

Personally, my neighborhood moms' Facebook group is a place where I am learning to engage—not to preach a sermon but to be a listening ear. It's amazing how many prayer requests people share in those spaces if we are actually listening. When a woman writes asking for a divorce lawyer, I pray that the Lord would restore her marriage. And when a GoFundMe page is shared to support someone facing medical bills or burial fees, I give what I can and pray for continued healing from illness or loss. God has used this season to shape my view of my Jerusalem and to love those around me without imposing my presence in their lives if uninvited.

When it comes to delaying our mission trips, let's be intentional in how we are actively deinstitutionalizing Western missions; let's take the transaction out of it and infuse the movement with the power of the Holy Spirit and the good news of the gospel. The American church would benefit greatly from having leaders who are not only filled with the joy that comes from knowing the hope of the gospel but also filled with the power of the Holy Spirit that gives new life. Instead of producing a mass influx of international super-heroes seeking self-actualization in the name of Jesus, let us make faithful, available, and teachable servants for the kingdom. This transformation cannot take place without a significant effort for the fundamentals of the Western per-spective on mission to be not only challenged but changed for good. For example, an emphasis on welcoming migrants and creating an avenue to listen and learn from the lived ex-periences of those in exile can disrupt the highly criticized and outdated missions movement. It's an easy step to take; our cities are full of diaspora communities that are struggling to make America their home for lack of hospitality from locals, especially those who consider themselves Christians. We can partner with their churches and build bridges to connect with the communities they represent to allow culturally rich exchanges between us and them. This type of connection forces Western Christians to step out of their comfort zones and break the barriers of racism, classism, and elitism that have plagued their communities. Experiencing God through another cultural lens also allows them to grow in awe and wonder of God's majesty as they see him work in other cultures.

These are the tools we must use to self-correct and silence the critics who rightfully call out the irony that the Western church that talks so much about the nations has ignored the people who represent those nations. Not only should the Western church be known for sending out missionaries, but she must lead the way by inviting in and receiving the "unlikely missionaries" from the Global South. Hospitality must be the most utilized tool for the next missions movement from the West. Hospitality should not be confused with having money; hospitality just needs a willing heart to provide a temporary refuge to someone in need by sharing what we have at the time. Hospitality doesn't politicize the struggles of Black and Brown people who are fleeing their home countries to save their lives and doesn't create a reason to disassociate oneself. Our mission movement must move to these places where the silence of the church has created a painful existence for people who are suffering injustices.

There are two layers to this that I want us Western Christians to consider. I believe the first question we must answer is, As individuals, will we stay and become a witness in our Jerusalem before pursuing going to Judea, Samaria, and the ends of the earth? For those who are leading the movement, churches, and mission organizations, Will you welcome those God has sent to revitalize your theology and mission? It is, in fact, a very difficult thing to consider staying when all you've been taught is to go; it's also difficult to receive when your whole existence lies in your ability to send. Nevertheless, if the West is to keep playing a vital role in mission, it's essential that we move away from a mission of doing and embrace a mission of being.

Charity is great, but it is only a vehicle to share the gospel. Charity without the sacrificial outworking of the gospel is just patronizing, well-meaning pity. Reducing communities to what they don't possess financially and exposing their vulnerability to the world in the name of addressing their spiritual needs is dehumanization of God's most valuable creation. We must learn and value the use of heavenly metrics to do heavenly work. How do we expect to please the God who says it's impossible to please him without faith by crunching numbers and telling distorted stories that dishonor his work in humanity? Our approach to measuring the success of our missional strategies needs to be oriented toward relational legacies being built wherever we go. The West, in fact, has a hidden gem in historically Black churches who have mastered the art of backyard ministry and an integrity in embracing hospitality. While Western evangelical churches that are majority white consider staying, they must not confuse their need to stay with a need to engage in "urban ministry" in Black communities; what's needed is to focus on racial justice and reconciliation.

THE BLACK CHURCH'S MISSIONAL MOVEMENT

Today a diversity and inclusion effort is slowly growing in historically white institutions, many of which were part of Jim Crow. Obviously this move to diversity and inclusion won't be successful without people of color leading the way. It also will not succeed without the African American church that has historically been a leader in seeking justice, peace, and reconciliation and continues to model the way today. Although predominantly white churches haven't been keen on following her lead, the Black church continues to be an example of forgiveness and perseverance. The attempt to create diversity without actually seeking forgiveness from the historically oppressed church in America would be foolishness for God's people. It will continue to tokenize Black and Brown people for the purpose of saving face in a politically charged time and creating more pain and division. More importantly, it will not produce the character needed to be gospel carriers around the globe. In order to understand the gravity of the oppression Black Christians endured in evangelicalism, we must look at history.

According to Vaughn Walston and Robert Stevens, "In some countries in Africa, black missionaries were not welcome. South Africa utilized obstructive tactics and legislation to exclude black missions, which they considered dangerous to the Bantu. In other nations, blacks were excluded for fear they would spread 'Garveyism,' the subversive belief in 'Africa for the Africans.'"[4] This is no small issue. It's worth noting that it was the white South African apartheid leaders who made sure Black missionaries wouldn't enter the country. If they did, they feared, they would embolden the African people to overthrow white supremacy. Even today there aren't that many Black Americans being sent on the mission field, even though it's an opportune time for Africans and those of African descent to benefit from their leadership in standing against injustice.

During Jim Crow, Black missionaries were called back to return from the mission field, which makes the church not only complicit but actively racist toward Black missionaries. It also makes missions a vehicle that supported the expansion of injustice on the African continent.

Dr. Linda Saunders explains that racism is a recurring theme throughout the Protestant ministry movement, revealing its dark side:

As evidenced through established laws, the cultural trajectory of American society and the eventual segregation of religious organizations based solely upon racist agendas, the protestant missionary movement strained under the weight of racialized inequality. The cancer of racism infected and infested the entire global missions endeavor forcing the pioneers of the Protestant missionary movement—the African-American church—to abandon her missional post.[5]

This shows us that the Black church in America has been forced to stay and has been forbidden from fulfilling the Great Commission as God intended. Yet when the issue of the lack of Black missionaries is brought up, many in missiology culture neglect to point this fact out and instead shift the blame to Black pastors and leaders and their inability to inspire their congregation to go.

In fact, the Black church is no stranger to producing amazing missionaries. A prime example of a Black missionary is Rebekka Protten, who contextualized the gospel in a way that honored and reached her people. Dr. Saunders writes:

The European's view of the African slave contributed to the demoralization and negative portrayal of enslaved Blacks. Africans were stripped of their cultural identity, thereby rendering them less than human and without moral and spiritual value. Protten challenged the status quo of her era as she began to teach slaves—not just spiritual lessons, but temporal lessons as well. She gave them access to education by teaching them to read, write and do simplistic mathematical computations. When their educational access was threatened by the burning of their books and constant moral degradation, Protten—and other Negroes—intervened to the king of Denmark on behalf of the slaves. Through spiritual and temporal education, Rebekka Protten elevated a less than marginalized people to the status of their masters, thereby rendering them equal to their masters. Rebekka's audacious attempt to insist on dignity for the slave community set the Negro converts on the same plateau as the white missionary. Thus, it can be argued, the gospel was placed in an appropriate setting—contextualized—because the slaves were allowed to embrace a new spiritual and temporal identity.[6]

Rebekka Protten is just one example of the many Black missionaries who against all odds have made an eternal impact for the kingdom. That impact was not only spiritual but also a physical one for those these missionaries interacted with. The theology of the Black church was and still is robust in its pursuit of justice and fighting oppression that has a physical and spiritual impact on humankind. As such, the value Black missionaries add to the Western missions movement is no secret. Therefore, their lack of their involvement in the current movement should be alarming and something that needs extreme attention. We need to be led by those who understand what being marginalized is like so that we can do away with self-serving attempts to connect with those on the margins. The global church needs the Black church's tried and true biblical method of suffering and faithful perseverance in times of atrocity as countries are being torn apart by war, genocide, and tribalism. This is one more reason for the Western church to stop sending those with no experience or applicable skills and to invest in learning from and sending Black Christians.

AVOID TOKENIZING PEOPLE OF COLOR

As the need to send Black and Brown missionaries becomes apparent, we must be aware that they will still be seen as outsiders to the receiver. Although they won't have the weight of being white and seen as a savior on them, they will still be seen as an outsider.

> When Black Missionaries were sent in the past it was under the belief that the black were better able to endure the rigors of the African tropics, which was something of a myth. They were recruited for their "ability to endure Africa" and for their cultural adaptability. It was the opinion of George Washington Carver that "American blacks" in their language and religion and customs are American, as much so as Europeans who have come here from the earliest day to the present time. Kermit Overton says "upon my arrival in this country, the Africans gave me the impression that they expected me to take up their habits, customs and language without difficulty. . . . After a while they concluded that I was not one of them. The result is that they accepted me as any other missionary and other testimonies of black missionaries being called "that black white lady's work."[7]

In Ethiopia we use the word *ferenje* to describe a foreigner. Although the original meaning of the word describes a white foreigner, we use it interchangeably to describe any other foreigners as well, sort of like how Overton described "that black white lady's work." Attempting to hire Black and Brown people to do missions in historically all-white institutions with all-white theology and all-white leadership will only exploit those Black and Brown Christians, exposing them to further alienation and displacement on the mission field. The Black missional movement cannot be expected to grow out of white institutions, but it can be celebrated, supported, and championed by those institutions. Collaboration and unity come from a place of accepting the history, theology, strategy, and witness of a community without an attempt to whitewash it so it's acceptable to a white audience.

The founder of Be the Bridge, Latasha Morrison, often speaks about how Black people are not a monolithic group of people, that we have different cultures and we are diverse within ourselves. I fear there is a romanticizing of the Black missionary in the West because the days of the white missionary being welcomed as a hero are over, and institutions that don't want to become irrelevant are thinking they need to recruit more Black people. Unless historically white methodology and practices change, it won't matter who goes, because people will still know they're getting the same approach with different faces.

> The Black experience in America will give the black missionary a unique perspective on a variety of situations. A common practice that Black missionaries might be particularly offended by is exclusivism among missionaries. As I talk to missionaries serving on various fields, I learn that the missionary subculture still excludes national Christians from many activities and conveniences

in many subtle ways. To Black Americans, this is reminiscent of the old Jim Crow laws in the South, or apartheid in South Africa. The Black experience in America has made our race sensitive to issues, attitudes and practices that offend nonwestern people. While missionaries often must be told that something is offensive, the Black missionary may already have an innate awareness of this. Because of this, an integrated missions force can help mission organizations better perceive subtle acts of discrimination that can hinder the Gospel.[8]

Sending missionaries who have a cultural, racial, and socioeconomic awareness of what it means to be on the margins only makes their integration into the communities they go to that much easier. They can empathize better; they have a natural ability to navigate situations where they're not the dominant voice, and this allows them to easily learn and be led before they attempt to lead. This obviously applies to everyone who has lived their lives as a cultural minority or those who are bicultural. It does not exclude white people; it just shrinks the pool we recruit from if our emphasis is cultural competency rather than an ability to raise money. In order to restore what's broken, we need to examine what is broken at the heart of the issue before we attempt to fix it. I'm talking about a truly reformed approach to missions that's not tempted to lean on power, money, influence, and mobilizing the masses, an approach that doesn't harm Black and Brown people in the name of the gospel. We must be careful not to allow history to repeat itself and to distance ourselves from the association of the gospel with colonialism.

A male white leader once told me that he's so used to being the leading voice in a room that if the conversation doesn't require his input or if he's invited in only as a spectator, he doesn't feel comfortable sitting and listening. In other words, he doesn't take part in conversations that don't center his experience. He was humbly admitting that he didn't know how to sit under the leadership of local international pastors as he started his racial identity journey. I was struck by two things: one, his humility in admitting this reality, and two, how the enemy had robbed him of learning from other cultures and taking in the beauty of seeing God in his glory fully expressed in other cultures. As much as I celebrate my friend's journey and growth, it would be dangerous for a person of color to be under his leadership without a policy of open accountability and transparency. My friend was in charge of a budget that consisted of millions of dollars and how that money would be used in the mission field locally and globally.

These types of conversations must be had in many of our organizations, and leaders must self-identify where they are in their understanding of justice and how that impacts their decision making. We have to start asking the right questions such as: Why are white evangelicals the only group of Christians who lead, influence, and shape the Western missions movement? What are the obstacles that prevent people of color from joining this movement? How can those from the Global South benefit by sending a culturally, racially, and socioeconomically conscious missionaries?

On the other hand, Black missionaries have to navigate many layers of culture with white leaders while attempting to do crosscultural ministry in another part of the world. They must manage cultural differences, interpret coded language, and endure microaggressions from "well-intentioned" colleagues, all while learning another language and culture. It's impossible to excel in a culturally oppressive organizational culture while still trying to do crosscultural ministry. It's exhausting and completely understandable why we don't see many people of color as missionaries supported under these institutions. Therefore, sending organizations must do their racial reconciliation work and create an inclusive environment where people of color can thrive because they are an asset to this movement that has long overlooked them. The future of mission from the West lies in our ability to mobilize the next generation of Christians who are diverse and bicultural.

TEN

A JUST MISSION

We must all learn to live together as brothers,
or we will all perish together as fools.

MARTIN LUTHER KING JR.

THE MORE I STAYED in predominantly white institutions and advanced in my leadership role, the more impatient I grew with the lack of mutuality and respect for the leadership of those from the Global South. Although the desire for collaboration might be there, the lack of action tells me that the Western church doesn't necessarily see the urgency. Pastor and author David P. Cassidy says:

> The average Christian in the world is not male but female, not white but brown or black, third world, not first world, far more Pentecostal than Presbyterian. The "average" Christian in the world today is a 22-year-old brown female. She has not been to your conference, she has not read CS Lewis or *Christianity Today*; she has not read your blog, nor mine, and does not go to Starbucks

or care one bit about alternative endings to *Game of Thrones* or if the latest lyric from Hillsong agrees with our confessional standards.[1]

If our expectation for those like this twenty-two-year-old Brown female is to carry a legacy left by white saviorism then we are misguided. The lived experience of Brown and Black Christians doesn't give them an opportunity to play the savior and therefore cannot continue on a legacy that was left behind. The mission movement for people of color looks different as they endure systemic racism, war, immigration, and generational poverty. The expectation that we will somehow use the same old approach and give it a facelift while hiding the legacy of injustice around missions is unrealistic. Seeking to build a justice-centric missional movement is not something we can put off any longer. Besides, the next generation of Western Christians cannot be persuaded to take on the mantle that has not put into practice their very heartbeat for justice.

Research provides further support for these types of views among young people. According to Barna:

> Engaged churchgoing Christians 18 to 34 appear to be more concerned than older adults with problematic aspects of the past. (It's worth mentioning here that, in Barna's experience, teen responses often look like their parents'; when they move into young adulthood, however, their views start to diverge more from previous generations' as they form their own opinions.) One-third of young adult Christians (34%) agree that "in the past, missions work has been unethical," compared

to one in four adults 35 and older (23%). Two in five (42%) agree that "Christian mission is tainted by its association with colonialism" (vs. 29% older adults 35+, 31% teens).[2]

It seems that young adults are more willing than older generations to raise questions about the ethics of missions and the lack of teaching around justice as the heart of the gospel. I am hopeful to see the dedication for truth and justice in them and thankful for the work the Lord is doing. They are unapologetically seeking to honor God with everything they cosign on, and the Western mission movement is not on the list. It would be a great disservice to God and his kingdom to not link arms with those on the frontlines of this work. As alarming as this may be for some who see the old way as the good way, I want to assure you that this is necessarily the step we must take to build a more inclusive missional movement.

As the Western church avoids true reconciliation, young people—Christians and non-Christians—are getting closer to the answer of unity and reconciliation as they seek truth and justice. The response of the church is vital to their heartbeat. Will we champion a tokenized mission movement lead by Black and Brown faces that perpetuates more of the same or will we allow them to truly lead us so reconciliation and restoration take place? We must steer clear from inviting Black and Brown people to lead organizations that have perpetuated white saviorism for decades only to burden them with "saving" their legacies. Instead seek them out to create a diverse and collaborative effort that includes everyone's voice. Let us avoid advocating for a facelift but truly undergo a transformative change that starts with reconciling the past with the present and that leads to a collective repentance.

This will mean the end of white saviorism and its struggle to remain at the center of the mission movement God has designed to be diverse. We can do God's work without institutionalizing the gospel and be free from the power dynamics that entangle us. We can undertake a mission movement that is marked by believers who are persecuted for the kingdom and whose stories, although not celebrated on earth, are written in the book of life, with one audience saying, "Good and faithful servant."

There may be at times no earthly metrics to measure and celebrate these missionaries' successes—no annual board meetings, no support money coming in—but God's name is still being proclaimed. The gospel is being preached in detention centers at the border, in jails, in a mud hut, and in the middle of fleeing one's country because of war and terror. These individuals may not have an annual salary or a financial support system but receive their manna directly from heaven and earn their food from the work of the gospel. I can hear the critics saying, "What's wrong with metrics? Metrics are good; we need to measure and record so we know how to do better." Yes, metrics are good if you're trying to build an institution, but not when you're trying to empower individuals to run freely with the gospel. Unless Western believers acknowledge that God has been and will continue to lead a missional movement that has nothing to do with their strategies, mission statements, and metrics, I fear they will fail to see the big picture.

The only way we can take part in God's work is if we, too, are taken by his mighty power and marvel at his majesty. We cannot direct, execute, strategize, and evangelize if our mission has no life in it. The risen Savior is beyond our scope and our strategies. He cannot be held back because borders are closed. He is a God who reveals himself through visions and dreams to those who have no access to the Bible. He has no bounds, and it is our greatest honor to be invited in this journey of spreading the gospel around the world. Let's give glory where glory is due and join him where his Spirit calls us to go.

The new generation of missionaries is justice seeking and gospel believing. They are rising up to build a beautiful future for the global church. They understand that the church's strength is in its people coming together to form a union that supports each other's work but doesn't conform to each other's ways. They are a true picture of the body of Christ, with the ear doing the listening while the hand lifts up the weak and the feet go where needed. For everyone to function as a healthy organism in a way that beautifies the bride of Christ, true mutuality must be more than what it's been in the past. It must go beyond raising money for people in faraway lands.

CONFRONTING GLOBAL INJUSTICE

Western Christians are in a unique position to use their voices for the oppressed around the globe and hold their elected officials accountable for many atrocities the West involves itself in. God's church cannot be silent as systemic poverty is being waged around the world.

Proxy war is one tool used against economically growing countries to keep them from flourishing. Understanding these issues will better equip us to stand for justice in the areas of the world where we seek to take the gospel. According to global policy analysts Candace Rondeaux and David Sterman, "Across the board, proxy warfare is generally conceptualized as a strategy in which one party encourages or uses another party to engage in warfare for its own strategic ends. At the crux of proxy warfare—in its many definitions— is the existence of a principal-agent relationship in the context of war."[3] Today's proxy war battlegrounds are unfortunately African and Middle Eastern countries that are coincidentally in the 10/40 window. While the two political powerhouses that are at odds are China and the West, we must ask why it is these other countries that are impacted. The struggle for economic power between China and the West affects the most vulnerable and takes innocent lives as collateral damage. Capitalism builds its wealth at the cost of the innocent blood of Black and Brown people, and this is not a part of our conversation when we urge people to go "on mission." Social media and news agencies owned by the one percent feed us information that demonizes Black and Brown people and paints them as primitives who senselessly kill each other. They cite ethnocentrism and terrorism as reasons for the conflict while omitting to say the real stakeholders are engineering the war and providing weapons for people groups to kill each other.

The destabilization of democracy in growing economies sets the development of those countries backward and opens wide doors for dead aid to come in and white saviorism to flourish. This is no light subject we can gloss over—as Christians we can make a substantial impact on the foreign policies being introduced and voted on in Congress by our own elected representatives. As Western believers we hold the most powerful tool in the world because we have the power to vote for fair and just leaders. As we vigorously search for these leaders, we must also consider the impact voting for them will have on the livelihood of those affected by their foreign policy. We have a godly responsibility to stand for issues concerning not only America but the globe. When we do that, there will be less reason for us to orient our missional goals toward damage control in situations our votes could have prevented in the first place.

A just mission has to be holistic and multidimensional, utilizing the power of the gospel to bridge the gap in equality and peace around the globe. We can work across faiths and denominations, cultures and languages when we start unifying around the basic human need for peace and justice as our common goal. Our presence will not be a threat to another's existence if we do our due diligence to proclaim the gospel in a society we respect and genuinely care for. We can collaborate better when we stop demonizing each other and learn to take others' experiences at face value rather than trying to convince them to see things our way. We will be much better at training future leaders of the global church when we see God's people as a mosaic of beautiful diversity. We must be a church that understands her calling to disciple everyone and remain faithful to her King by pointing us to say, "Maranatha—come, our Lord."

THE NEW GENERATION OF MISSION

God is working in ways we haven't experienced and in places we are not expecting. My work has given me the privilege of collecting stories of amazing diaspora leaders from around the globe. I cannot emphasize the need for us to prepare our hearts to see God's work outside our context. Our willingness and ability to listen to stories like the ones I will share in the next few pages will determine our success in creating a united mission movement. Mehari is an Ethiopian missionary to the United States who shared with me about a friend of his, saying, "I have been praying with her and discipling her long distance. Now she feels called to start a home church in your neighborhood." The story got more beautiful as Mehari shared with me how he met this lovely woman on a plane, and while they were chatting, he shared the gospel with her. They exchanged numbers and kept in touch as he continued to guide her spiritually from a distance. Although he lived on the West Coast at the time, he kept up with her journey, and when he found out I lived near her, he called to connect us.

I was struck by the beautiful things happening in this encounter. My friend, an Ethiopian man, had a purely spiritual and shepherding relationship with a white American woman that led her to start a home church. She was not only transformed spiritually but also willing to turn around and follow God's call on her life to serve him. My friend was able to empower a woman to take on a ministry role that many in her culture would have discouraged her from because in our culture it was not an issue. A woman starting a home church would be a no-no for many pastors in America, but not for Mehari. I marvel at the beautiful display of God's love and care for this woman to encounter a spiritual leader who was not shaped or intimidated by cultural barriers that would have held her back from following God's call to reach the nations. Mehari helped her grow in her faith exponentially because there were no cultural barriers that prevented him from seeing her as an equal partner in the gospel.

I am encouraged to see people like José, a church planter, who was born in America and raised in El Salvador. His father pastored a church there after moving back home to serve his community, then José moved back to America for seminary and ended up planting a multicultural church in Charlotte, North Carolina. When he launched his church we worked together on a project for our community. His goal was clear: to provide opportunities beyond church activities for the Latino community in Charlotte. We developed a training program that intertwined discipleship with entrepreneurship opportunities for youth. We both knew too well that kids who looked like us had too many financial and social burdens to be trained solely in vocational ministry. They needed to be able to earn an income that would support their families.

Most second-generation immigrant kids have to support their parents, themselves, and their siblings. In some cases, they eventually send money back home to grandparents or extended relatives. They cannot survive on a ministry salary. If we want these believers to use their gifts to build the kingdom of God, we have to make sure they're able to create other streams of income. Entrepreneurship as a model of mission—one that must be embraced by organizations that want to be multicultural—was our goal. We knew financial independence would help our immigrant community members not to fear full-time ministry as an economic risk. I am thankful for leaders like José who are building these initiatives in their churches. I can't wait to see the strong disciples and entrepreneurs these kids will become in the next ten years or so. What a legacy they'll be leaving for their own kids and what a legacy José has already left by taking a risk and planting a church that serves the underserved.

A couple of years ago while searching for African missionaries to connect with, I stumbled upon an article by Diana Nkhoma, a young Malawian missionary with Young Life, and reached out to her. She shared with me about her passion for young African believers who are struggling with their faith and their culture. She described the sense of betrayal they felt in the way missionaries had spread Christianity to their ancestors. These young Malawians now want to distance themselves from that legacy, and the only way they think they can do it is by abandoning their faith and going back to their ancestral belief systems. Most feel their culture has been stripped away and are trying to reconnect with their heritage. Meanwhile the faith that was given to them without any cultural sensitivity and contextualization seems foreign, and they don't want to have anything to do with it.

Diana has a passion to step in the middle and reclaim the gospel as culturally and historically African. She has been studying ancient Christianity in Ethiopia and Egypt and desires to visit these historical sites. As I hear her story, I think about the work Dr. Vince Bantu is doing here in the United States to reclaim the gospel (*bisrat*) and show its African roots for the African American Christians who are struggling with the same issues African Christians are struggling with. For people like Diana who want to experience Christianity without the influence of colonialism, the work of redemptive storytelling will include visiting ancient African churches like the Lalibela in Ethiopia. God is bigger than our tainted view of him and bigger than our mistakes, and we must join him in spreading the news that Christianity is *not* a white man's religion.

Josh is another friend who reached out to me a few years ago after reading my rebuttal to an article about why Africa needs more Western missionaries. He is one of the pastors of a church in Arizona and leads a beautiful ministry called the Daniel Initiative. Josh, a white millennial pastor in a fairly large church, understands the need for his church to learn from immigrant pastors. He believes immigrant churches are the voice of reason for the Western church just as Daniel was for Babylon. He seeks out pastors from different cultures and gives them a platform to teach, fellowship together, and lead in their respective spaces. As a white pastor, he knows his role for the most part is to listen, champion their vision, and raise funds on their behalf.

I love working with Josh because he is the epitome of a true partner in the faith. No topic is off-limits for Josh. He pursues truth and seeks reconciliation because he understands that the cost is too great for the kingdom of God if he looks away. When I ask him what his biggest takeaway has been from working with international pastors, he says, "Praying with them is one of the most spiritually reviving and beautiful experiences I've ever had, and I will give anything to be at their feet seeking God out with them." We need more Joshes. If the Western church can focus on producing disciples like Josh, we will do amazing work for the kingdom together.

There are others like Naomi who, more than a decade living in America pursuing a successful career as an IT project manager, with a physician husband and two beautiful daughters, decided to visit her home. While on vacation she got invited to visit an orphanage a family member had started. She admits as she tells the story that the last thing she wanted to do was go to an orphanage and be sad at the conclusion of her happy vacation. But after visiting the orphanage and meeting the kids, her life changed. Two years later she and her husband adopted twin boys and welcomed them into their family. Now living in McLean, Virginia, they lead an orphan care movement in Ethiopia that goes beyond adoption. They've created "a sustainable model that is now caring for orphans through volunteers in Ethiopia. [Orphan Care Ethiopia] works with local communities, other nonprofits, and Ethiopian local and national governments to address the orphan challenge in Ethiopia through domestic adoption, advocacy, and education."[4] Naomi had no ministry training nor an ounce of desire to adopt children five years ago, but as she puts it, "God had other plans."

Last but not least, one of the most impactful ministries in my life has been led by a Rwandan genocide survivor, Dr. Celestin Musekura. He started ALARM (African Leadership and Reconciliation Ministry) Inc. with the intention of training African leaders for biblical reconciliation. After losing his family to the horrendous genocide in his country, he found Christ, who changed his life and gave him the mission to forgive his offenders and reconcile the nation. When I first learned about ALARM, I called the organization and expressed my desire to learn more about it. I was given Dr. Musekura's direct number and told that he had an open-door policy with African leaders, that I was welcome to contact him and set up a time to talk. That phone call has changed my life by showing me that Africa in fact does have incredibly capable leaders such as Dr. Musekura who understand how reconciliation works. His wisdom and experience, which should be sought out here in the West as churches try to navigate forgiveness and justice, is underutilized. We should pursue people like him to sit under as well as reading their books and listening to their sermons. We need more ministries like ALARM and reconcilers like Dr. Musekura— people who have lived through what a lot of communities are experiencing today and can lead them to Christ with great care through their suffering.

God works in multidimensional and ever-changing ways with people who are willing to go with him wherever he will send them. I share these stories as a way to challenge our one-size-fits-all model. Missional strategies must be as diverse as the cultures and worlds they operate in. We cannot export a top-down model from comfortable Western boardrooms and expect it to work. The smaller the model, the more agile it will be and easier to mold and shape after God's heart. Our exposure is limited to our experiences, therefore our methods will vary. Because I am from a particular culture and geographical location in the world, my exposure has largely been with African missionaries and their work. Nevertheless I am inspired by the works of people like Michelle Reyes, the vice president of the Asian American Christian Collaborative, and Vivian Mabuni, author and host of the *Someday Is Here* podcast. These women are doing amazing work to elevate the voices of Asian Americans and highlight their work in the kingdom. I have so much to learn from their stories and how their culture informs their worship of God.

In every culture we find that God has wonderful and capable people working tirelessly for his kingdom to be proclaimed above all else. It's a privilege to find and connect with those who have a unique call to their own people. Just as Nehemiah was called to strategically build his people's faith and physical well-being, God has seated many believers around us here in the United States and around the world. Our attempt to seek them out and learn from them will only fuel our passion to pursue the God of nations.

A CALL TO TRUE UNITY

One of the earliest defiances by collective humankind was its attempt to overthrow God from his throne by building the tower of Babel. The desire to be like him and reach his glory resembled Satan's desire to be like him. Because of their attempt to unify around an evil mission, God decided to confuse their language and destroy their plan. That is why we must fiercely fight the demonic powers of sameness that reveal themselves through white supremacy and nationalism, whether it be a political party or denominational alliances that try to pull us away from our true calling to be stamped by the gospel and proclaim truth and justice at any cost beyond party lines and borders. Anything that tries to impose uniformity of theology and culture and attempts to demean the beauty found in God's diverse church must be rejected. Of course, there is beauty in having a denominational background and heritage. I love my Ethiopian evangelical upbringing, but I don't die on the hill of protecting it if it stands in the way of truth and justice and my ability to understand and support God's people.

The Western church has a lot of work to do in her attempt to rebuild her fractured walls. As God gave Nehemiah the wisdom to delegate the work to each tribe, the Western church must delegate to God's multiethnic children. That is the only way the wall can be kept up, maintained, and cared for. We cannot do it alone while separated and segregated.

God created us for community and with a desire to live harmoniously together. Yet instead of true multiethnic and complex unity, we choose easy, simple, self-affirming monolithic unity that serves us and our interests. We believe the lie that if everyone looks, speaks, and thinks like us, we will finally belong and feel at home. In reality, true community is one that is difficult and a path that sanctifies us to abandon our self-interest and pursue God's heart. So let us seek a just mission, by willingly laying down power and embracing mutuality.

ACKNOWLEDGMENTS

THIS BOOK WOULD HAVE BEEN IMPOSSIBLE without the love and support of my family and friends.

To my husband, Ermias, thank you for challenging me to think outside the box and not to settle. You are God's reminder of how beautiful the culture he gave us is; thank you for teaching me to honor God by honoring where I came from. I am forever grateful that you lead our family gently.

To my two gifts, my children, Natania Ermias (my little theologian) and Noah Ermias, you inspired me to wrestle with the issues in this book. It would be a tragedy to miss out on an opportunity to teach you God's beauty through his creation and all the many cultures he's made. He is magnificent, and as you seek him out you will embark on the majesty of the King.

To Dr. Abeneazer Urga, thank you for believing in this passion project, for tirelessly praying for me and for directing me toward countless resources. Your encouragement has meant the world during this writing process.

To Michele Dudley, thank you for standing in my corner and allowing me to express my frustrations with the mission movement while gently nudging me to think of solutions—we need more of you.

To Latasha Morrison and Be the Bridge, thank you for the work you do to create a path for reconciliation and unity. Your work helped me find my voice and I am eternally grateful.

To the countless mentors, supporters, and encouragers the Lord has allowed my path to intersect with, thank you for seeing God's work in my life and speaking truth with love. The body of Christ has truly loved me, and I pray my love is reflected in this work.

Thank you, InterVarsity Press, for believing in the message and opening the door for me to share my perspective boldly.

To my agent, Jevon Bolden, who championed this work from the beginning and believed in the message God gave me to share to his church, thank you for believing in me. We did it!

QUESTIONS FOR REFLECTION AND DISCUSSION

1. THE AWAKENING

1. How did your upbringing prepare you to live a culturally conscious life?

2. In what ways does racism impact our ability to share the gospel effectively with all people?

3. Why would a Christian be persuaded to seek justice for all if their life hasn't allowed them to experience injustice personally?

2. THE MISSIONARY

1. Would you consider yourself a missionary? Why or why not?

2. How have your views on how to share the gospel with people from other cultures been shaped in the past?

3. Is there anything you'll do differently moving forward?

3. THE DOCTRINE OF DISCOVERY

1. How has your training in crosscultural ministry affected the way you view people from other cultures?

2. Is there a single story that you believe about a group of people that needs to be challenged?

3. What is your experience with cultural norms being violated in mission work?

4. CONTEXTUALIZING THEOLOGY

1. How has your denominational background shaped your view of other belief systems?

2. What aspects of the topic of the gifts of the Spirit do you find difficult to navigate?

3. How has your theological view impacted your ability to be in a mutual community with believers from other cultures?

5. DECOLONIZING SHORT-TERM MISSION

1. If you've been on a short-term mission trip, what was your experience of mutuality and power like?

2. What are some intentional ways you can influence the economy of a community you've visited in the past?

3. How can you become a better mutual partner in the short-term mission movement? What can you do to break the power dynamic?

6. THE SACRED COW: MONEY

1. Who has God placed in your community as *yene bete* or "my kind of human" for you to meet their physical needs?

2. How does horizontal giving challenge your view of Western philanthropy?

3. What are some practical ways you can start seeking community with those from other cultural, socio-economic, and faith backgrounds?

7. RESTORATIVE JUSTICE

1. What's your understanding of global politics in relation to mission?

2. What are some conscious decisions you can make to move away from harmful practices of mission?

3. How would you reverse the brain drain that forces people to migrate to the West and live as exiles?

8. THE FUTURE OF MISSION

1. What or who has the conversation of racial reconciliation in the church cost you?

2. What are some ways you can ensure that the nations are represented at the leadership level of organizations that aim to reach the world?

3. What is the unique opportunity the diaspora Christian community possesses for the expansion of the gospel? How can you utilize that?

9. A REASON TO STAY

1. What are some ways you can redirect your global mission efforts that have been harmful so that they become helpful?

2. What type of role do you think the Black church can play in the next phase of the mission movement?

3. Why is there a need to pursue reconciliation with the Black church before focusing on world mission? What is your role in it?

10. A JUST MISSION

1. What steps can you take to confront global injustices and stand in the gap?

2. How does reading the many stories of missionaries shared in this chapter challenge your view of mission?

3. Will you commit to living a multiethnic life that births a multiethnic church and a just mission?

NOTES

1. THE AWAKENING

[1]Beverly Daniel Tatum, *Why Are All the Black Kids Sitting Together in the Cafeteria? And Other Conversations about Race* (New York: Basic Books, 2017), 135.

[2]"Missions Stats: The Current State of the World," The Traveling Team, updated November 2021, www.thetravelingteam.org/stats.

[3]Philip Hunt, "Why Africa Still Needs Western Workers," July 13, 2017, The Gospel Coalition, www.thegospelcoalition.org/article/why-africa-still-needs-western-workers.

[4]"The Story of Africa: Christianity," BBC World Service, www.bbc.co.uk/worldservice/africa/features/storyofafrica/index_section8.shtml, accessed January 7, 2022.

2. THE MISSIONARY

[1]Greg Ogden, *Discipleship Essentials*, rev. ed. (Downers Grove, IL: InterVarsity Press, 2019).

[2]Greg Ogden, *Transforming Discipleship: Making Disciples a Few at a Time* (Downers Grove, IL: InterVarsity Press, 2003).

[3]George Müller, G. Fred Bergin, and Arthur T. Pierson, *Autobiography of George Müller: Or, a Million and a Half in Answer to Prayer* (Denton, TX: Westminster Literature Resources, 2003).

[4]Catherine M. Swift, *Gladys Aylward* (Minneapolis: Bethany House, 1989).

3. THE DOCTRINE OF DISCOVERY

[1]J. Oliver Conroy, "The Life and Death of John Chau, the Man Who Tried to Convert His Killers," *The Guardian*, February 3, 2019, www.theguardian.com/world/2019/feb/03/john-chau-christian-missionary-death-sentinelese.

[2]Mark Charles, "Doctrine of Discovery," Mark Charles for President, www.markcharles2020.com/doctrine-of-discovery, accessed January 9, 2022.

[3]This quote has also been attributed to a German play called *Der Stellvertreter. Ein christliches Trauerspiel* (translation: *The Deputy: A Christian Tragedy*) by Rolf Hochhuth, which has been translated into numerous languages. The quotation as presented is from Rolf Hochhuth, *The Deputy*, trans. Richard Winston and Clara Winston (New York: Grove Press, 1964), 144.

[4]"Religion in the Colonies," History Central, 2020, www.historycentral.com /TheColonies/Religion.html.

[5]Chimamanda Ngozi Adichie, "The Danger of a Single Story," TED, July 2009, www.ted.com/talks/chimamanda_ngozi_adichie_the_danger_of_a _single_story.

[6]F. A. Oborji, "Missiology in an African Context: Toward a New Language," *Missiology* 31, no. 3 (2003): 321-38.

4. CONTEXTUALIZING THEOLOGY

[1]Mark 16:9-20 is not recorded in some ancient manuscripts of Mark's Gospel, which presents a puzzle for theologians who study and specialize in early manuscripts.

[2]Philip Jenkins, *The New Faces of Christianity: Believing the Bible in the Global South* (New York: Oxford University Press, 2006), 103.

[3]Tibebe Eshete, *The Evangelical Movement in Ethiopia: Resistance and Resilience* (Waco, TX: Baylor University Press, 2017).

[4]Sean Illing, "The Brutal Mirror," Vox, November 2, 2019, www.vox.com/first -person/2018/2/19/16739386/ayahuasca-retreat-psychedelic-hallucination -meditation.

[5]Wesley Granberg-Michaelson, "Which Global Church? The Pentecostal World Fellowship and the WCC," *The Christian Century*, January 21, 2014, www .christiancentury.org/article/2014-01/which-global-church.

[6]Abeneazer Urga, "The Impact of the Enlightenment on Hermeneutics, Pneumatology and Demonology, and the Implications to Mission" (unpublished manuscript, 2019, Columbia, SC).

[7]Timothy C. Tennent, *Theology in the Context of World Christianity: How the Global Church Is Influencing the Way We Think About and Discuss Theology* (Grand Rapids, MI: Zondervan Academic, 2007).

[8]David Wells, "The Theologian's Craft," in *Doing Theology in Today's World*, ed. John D. Woodbridge and Thomas Edward McComiskey (Grand Rapids, MI: Zondervan, 1991), 172.

[9]T. C. Oden, *How Africa Shaped the Christian Mind: Rediscovering the African Seedbed of Western Christianity* (Downers Grove, IL: InterVarsity Press, 2010).

[10]Matt Smethurst and Bill Walsh, "Celebrating 10 Years of Theological Famine Relief," The Gospel Coalition, March 3, 2016, www.thegospelcoalition.org /article/celebrating-10-years-of-theological-famine-relief.

[11]John S. Mbiti, "Theological Impotence and Universality of the Church," in *Mission Trends No. 3: Third World Theologies*, ed. Gerald H. Anderson and Thomas F. Stransky (New York: Paulist Press, 1976), 17.

[12]David J. Bosch, *Witness to the World: The Christian Mission in Theological Perspective* (Atlanta: John Knox Press, 1980), 153-54.

[13]"Christian Millennials Are Most Likely Generation to Lean Toward Charismatic Worship," Barna Group, July 23, 2020, www.barna.com/research /worship-preferences.

5. DECOLONIZING SHORT-TERM MISSION

[1]Ivan Illich, "To Hell with Good Intentions," address to the Conference on InterAmerican Student Projects in Cuernavaca, Mexico, on April 20, 1968, University of Vermont, www.uvm.edu/~jashman/CDAE195_ESCI375/To %20Hell%20with%20Good%20Intentions.pdf.

[2]Christine Bednarz, "Inside the Controversial World of Slum Tourism," *National Geographic*, April 25, 2018, www.nationalgeographic.com/travel /article/history-controversy-debate-slum-tourism.

[3]"Reading: Maslow's Hierarchy of Needs," Lumen Learning, https://courses .lumenlearning.com/wmintrobusiness/chapter/reading-need-based -motivation-theories, accessed January 15, 2022.

[4]"Research and Statistics," ShortTermMissions.com, www.shortterm missions.com/articles/mission-trip-research, accessed January 15, 2022.

[5]"Short-Term Mission Trips: Are They Worth the Investment?" Baylor University Media and Public Relations, May 2, 2011, www.baylor.edu/media communications/news.php?action=story&story=93238.

[6]Harmen Jalvingh and Joris Postema, *Stop Filming Us*, directed by Joris Postema (Netherlands: Doxy Films, 2020).

[7]Evan Sparks, "The 'Great Commission' or Glorified Sightseeing?" WSJ Opinion, *Wall Street Journal*, October 10, 2008, www.wsj.com/articles /SB122359398873721053.

6. THE SACRED COW: MONEY

[1]A. C. Jemison, "Did You Know Black Ghettos Were Deliberately Created by Gov't Sponsored Redlining?" Urban Intellectuals, February 8, 2017,

https://urbanintellectuals.com/know-black-ghettos-deliberately-created-govt-sponsored-redlining.

[2]Emma Lazarus, "The New Colossus," Poetry Foundation, www.poetryfoundation.org/poems/46550/the-new-colossus, accessed January 22, 2022.

[3]Alexis Clark, "Tulsa's 'Black Wall Street' Flourished as a Self-Contained Hub in Early 1900s," History.com, January 27, 2021, www.history.com/news/black-wall-street-tulsa-race-massacre.

[4]Kidist Yasin, "Snapshot on Philanthropy in Ethiopia," Lilly Family School of Philanthropy, IUPUI, April 8, 2020, https://blog.philanthropy.iupui.edu/2020/04/08/snapshot-on-philanthropy-in-ethiopia.

[5]Lawrence J. Friedman and Mark D McGarvie, *Charity, Philanthropy, and Civility in American History* (New York: Cambridge University Press, 2002), 50.

[6]"What Is Social Business? Executive Factsheet," HEC Paris, www.hec.edu/en/faculty-research/centers/society-organizations-institute/think/so-institute-executive-factsheets/what-social-business, accessed January 21, 2022.

[7]Friedman and McGarvie, *Charity, Philanthropy, and Civility*, 241-42.

[8]Valaida Fullwood, *Giving Back: A Tribute to Generations of African American Philanthropists* (Charlotte, NC: Foundation for the Carolinas, 2011), 33.

[9]"Mexican Migrants Sent Home a Record $40 Billion in 2020," Associated Press, February 2, 2021, https://apnews.com/article/coronavirus-pandemic-mexico-d5cca3a4e77a258223bb4222f02496ad.

7. RESTORATIVE JUSTICE

[1]Nelson Mandela, "On Freedom: I Am Prepared to Die," statement to the Pretoria Supreme Court, United Nations, April 20, 1964, www.un.org/en/events/mandeladay/court_statement_1964.shtml.

[2]Linda Thomas-Greenfield, "The United States and Africa: Perception and Policy," Carnegie Connects, YouTube, August 5, 2020, www.youtube.com/watch?v=8vPWcoGu7kg.

[3]Dambisa Moyo, *Dead Aid: Why Aid Is Not Working And How There Is A Better Way For Africa* (New York: Penguin, 2010).

[4]Paul Kagame, "CNN: Paul Kagame talks about *Dead Aid* and China," YouTube, July 25, 2009, www.youtube.com/watch?v=GJ-CvQSsMF0.

[5]Joe Myers, "Which Are Africa's Biggest Exports?" World Economic Forum, May 10, 2016, www.weforum.org/agenda/2016/05/which-are-africas-biggest-exports.

[6]K. Kale Yu, "Purification Rites: Understanding Recent Social Movements as Religious Confession and Cleansing," Communicating Religion's Relevance:

82nd Annual Meeting of the Association for the Sociology of Religion (virtual conference), August 8-9, 2021.

[7]"Biblical Justice and Race Statement," Prayer & Action Justice Initiative, www.prayerandactioncoalition.org, accessed January 23, 2022.

[8]Daniel Hill, *White Awake: An Honest Look at What It Means to Be White* (Downers Grove, IL: InterVarsity Press, 2017), 7.

[9]Obianuju Ekeocha, "An African Woman's Open Letter to Melinda Gates," Pontifical Council for the Laity, www.laici.va/content/laici/en/sezioni /donna/notizie/an-african-woman-s-open-letter-to-melinda-gates.html, accessed January 23, 2022.

[10]Frédéric Docquier, "The Brain Drain from Developing Countries," IZA World of Labor, May 2014, https://wol.iza.org/uploads/articles/31/pdfs/brain -drain-from-developing-countries.pdf.

[11]Asad Badruddin, "Reverse the Brain Drain," Stanford Social Innovation Review, October 3, 2016, https://ssir.org/articles/entry/reverse_the_brain_drain.

[12]Aleksandar Olic, "Waterfall Project Management Methodology," Active Collab, May 24, 2017, https://activecollab.com/blog/project-management /waterfall-project-management-methodology.

[13]"Manifesto for Agile Software Development," Agile Manifesto, https:// agilemanifesto.org, accessed January 24, 2022.

8. THE FUTURE OF MISSION

[1]Peter Wehner, "The Scandal Rocking the Evangelical World," *The Atlantic*, June 7, 2021, www.theatlantic.com/ideas/archive/2021/06/russell-moore -sbc/619122.

[2]"Lamin Sanneh: The Future of Christian Missions in a Changing World," Cook School of Intercultural Studies Distinguished Speakers Series, Biola University, December 22, 2015, www.youtube.com/watch?v=49IycNs__KQ.

[3]George G. Hunter III, *The Celtic Way of Evangelism: How Christianity Can Reach the West . . . Again* (Nashville: Abingdon Press, 2000).

[4]Doug Pagitt, "Most Americans Favor Welcoming Immigrants. Why Don't Christians?" Opinion, Religion News Service, August 27, 2021, https:// religionnews.com/2021/08/27/most-americans-favor-welcoming-immigrants -why-dont-christians.

[5]Lily Kuo, "Africa's 'Reverse Missionaries' Are Bringing Christianity Back to the United Kingdom," QuartzAfrica, October 11, 2017, https://qz.com/africa /1088489/africas-reverse-missionaries-are-trying-to-bring-christianity-back -to-the-united-kingdom.

[6]"Evangelical Call for Restitution-Based Immigration Reform," Evangelical Immigration Table, https://evangelicalimmigrationtable.com/restitution, accessed January 24, 2022.

[7]Adelle M. Banks, "More Multiracial Churches Led by Black, Hispanic Pastors," Religion News Service, *Christianity Today*, January 17, 2020, www.christianitytoday.com/news/2020/january/more-multiracial-churches-black-hispanic-pastors-mosaix.html.

[8]Robert Chao Romero, *Brown Church: Five Centuries of Latina/o Social Justice, Theology, and Identity* (Downers Grove, IL: IVP Academic, 2020), 211-12.

9. A REASON TO STAY

[1]"A Year Out: How COVID-19 Has Impacted Practicing Christians," Barna, March 18, 2021, www.barna.com/research/a-year-out.

[2]Max Bearak and Rael Ombuor, "A Child Sex Abuser Evaded Justice in Kenya. Then an 'Ordinary Woman' Took Matters into Her Own Hands," *The Washington Post*, February 4, 2021, www.washingtonpost.com/world/2021/02/04/kenya-orphanage-child-abuse.

[3]Sarah Harman, "U.S. Citizen Went to Uganda to Help Kids. Now Her Charity Is Accused of Killing Them," NBC News, August 5, 2019, www.nbcnews.com/news/world/u-s-citizen-went-uganda-help-kids-now-her-charity-n1035211.

[4]Vaughn J. Walston and Robert J. Stevens, eds., *African-American Experience in World Mission: A Call Beyond Community*, rev. ed. (Chesapeake, VA: William Carey Library, 2012), xx.

[5]Linda P. Saunders, "Laying an Historical Foundation to Examine the African-American Church's Relationship to 21st Century Global Missions to Create a Contextualized Missions Training Model for Future Generations of African-American Missionaries," (PhD diss., Columbia International University, 2020), https://dissexpress.proquest.com/dxweb/doc/2419327800.html?FMT=AI&desc=Laying+an+Historical+Foundation+to+Examine+the+African-American+Church.

[6]Saunders, "Laying."

[7]Walston and Stevens, *African-American Experience*, 57.

[8]Walston and Stevens, *African-American Experience*, 82.

10. A JUST MISSION

[1]David Cassidy (@DPCassidyTKC), "The average Christian in the world is not male but female," Twitter, August 8, 2020, 5:14 p.m., https://twitter.com/DPCassidyTKC/status/1292222735897198593.

[2]"Young Christians Value Missions, but Question Its Ethics," Barna Group, July 16, 2020, www.barna.com/research/young-christians-value-missions.

[3]Candace Rondeaux and David Sterman, "Twenty-First Century Proxy Warfare: Confronting Strategic Innovation in a Multipolar World," New America, February 20, 2019, www.newamerica.org/international-security /reports/twenty-first-century-proxy-warfare-confronting-strategic-innovation -multipolar-world/conclusion.

[4]Naomi Haile, "Naomi's Story," Orphan Care Ethiopia, www.orphancareethiopia .org/about-us/naomi-s-story, accessed January 29, 2022.